Nahanni: the river guide

Disclaimer

Suggestions offered for travelling on the Nahanni are just that — suggestions. I assume no responsibility for the misuse of this information, nor the failure of individuals to adequately assess their outdoor skills and the threat from natural hazards. The decision to run a particular river, river section or rapid, or to hike or camp in a particular area lies solely with the individual. The South Nahanni, the Flat River and their tributaries are wilderness rivers and as such are not recommended for novice paddlers.

Front cover: Virginia Falls.
Back cover: Entering The Gate, Third Canyon.
Inset photo of Fourth Canyon rapids.

NAHANNI
the RIVER GUIDE

Peter Jowett

Acknowledgements

I would like to thank the people who helped make this book possible: the wardens from Nahanni National Park Reserve; Neil Hartling; Hal Morrison, Debbie Ladouceur and Dave Salayka who provided me with information and inspiration; my sister Jane who helped with editing. I owe a great deal of thanks to my brother Mike. When I was a young sprout, Mike helped me gain an appreciation for the wild areas of Canada. Doug Eastcott, Keith Morton, Mary Enright, Don Beckett, Gillean Daffern, The Glenbow Archives Calgary, and the British Columbia Archives and Records Service supplied a few of the photographs. The Northwest Territories Archives in Yellowknife gave information on place names. Most of all, thanks Jude for the patience, support and persistence to "get the damn thing done".

Published by Rocky Mountain Books
#4 Spruce Centre,
Calgary, Alberta T3C 3B3

Canadian Cataloguing in Publication Data
 Jowett, Peter, 1960-
  Nahanni : the river guide

  Includes index.
  ISBN 0-921102-23-2
  1. South Nahanni River (N.W.T.)--Guidebooks.
2. Canoes and canoeing--Northwest Territories--South Nahanni River--Guidebooks. 3. Rafting (Sports)--Northwest Territories--South Nahanni River--Guidebooks. I. Title.
FC4195.S6J69 1993   917.19'3   C93-091775-8
F1100.S6J69 1993

COMMITTED TO THE DEVELOPMENT OF CULTURE AND THE ARTS

The publisher wishes to acknowledge the assistance of Alberta Culture and Multiculturalism, The Alberta Foundation for the Arts and The Federal Department of Communications in the publication of this book.

Contents

Background to Nahanni National Park Reserve

In the 1920's the airplane had become the workhorse of the north. It allowed larger companies to more thoroughly explore the Nahanni area for minerals. Roads were built and airstrips. At one time, private entrepreneurs planned to establish a health spa at Kraus Hotsprings where visitors could also hunt for big game in Nahanni's "tropical valleys". Time passed and gradually the federal government exerted greater control over the area's resources.

In 1958, the South Nahanni was first considered as a candidate for the national park system. The proposal to have Virginia Falls and the Flat River developed into a mega hydro-electric project in the early 1960's spurred officials into "action". In 1969, park officials made a formal proposal for the area to receive national park status which was finally granted in February of 1971 after Prime Minister Pierre Trudeau had taken a trip down the river. My, doesn't the government work fast!

The goal of Canada's National Park system is to represent all 49 natural regions comprising the Canadian landscape. In Nahanni National Park Reserve a 4,766 square-kilometre strip along the South Nahanni and Flat Rivers preserves and protects the natural and cultural features representative of the Mackenzie Mountains. In 1978, the park was recognized for its international significance and designated a World Heritage Site which placed it in the same realm as other world renowned sites such as the Galapagos Islands. In 1987 the South Nahanni was declared a Canadian Heritage River.

Nahanni National Park will remain a reserve until its boundaries have been firmly established following the completion of native land claims. Hopefully, remarkable and fragile areas such as the Cirque of the Unclimbables, Tlogotsho Plateau, and the karst landforms located north of First Canyon will then be included and protected within the park.

If you wish to help preserve these precious areas write to the Minister of the Environment at: Terraces de la Chaudiere, 284 10 Wellington Street, Hull, Quebec, K1A 0H3.

National Park Regulations

There are several regulations concerning visitor activity which are designed to protect the park and its resources. Generally, nothing is to be removed from the park and nothing harmed, with the exception of fish for which you need a licence. These regulations have a spirit behind them that should be applied to all natural areas in which you travel. Basically they reflect the old sentiment "take nothing but pictures; leave nothing but footprints."

Please note that under Territorial legislation, historic artifacts cannot be disturbed or taken from the park or from anywhere else in the Northwest Territories.

Foreword

I feel myself pivot in my seat as the waters of the Liard slip silently beneath the canoe. The air is crisp and clean with an expectant hint of the approaching autumn. The Butte is just a bump on the horizon now, framed in the rosy glow of yet another Nahanni sunset. As if on wing, I lift into the air and retrace my route up the river...The Splits, Deadmen Valley, the falls...What? Oh, oh, where am I? Has anyone noticed? Once again my mind has slipped back into itself and into another Nahanni daydream. For the briefest of seconds a sense of melancholy sweeps over me then just as quickly it's replaced with a satisfying feeling of having been so fortunate to have visited Nahanni.

In many respects Nahanni was my classroom, the place where I learned valuable lessons about both myself and the world in which I live. It taught me self-reliance, to trust my own physical and mental capabilities as I patrolled its remote and sometimes hazardous outer reaches. I learned to tune my senses to the surrounding environment, and to rely upon those senses for my well-being.

During my time there I met many people who had come to experience the magic of the area. These were people who, in general, shared the same love and respect I hold for our natural environment. But, even so, I perceived a problem; they weren't getting the whole story — the Nahanni story. So, I wrote this book. I wanted to provide fellow travellers with the information they need to gain a true respect for this magnificent place.

I also had another reason for writing this book. After working for a variety of national and provincial parks, I have come to some troubling conclusions. It's obvious that Canada's natural environment is going to hell-in-a-handbasket and we must not rely on the relatively small area represented by our national parks to maintain a healthy environment. Our parks are constantly being bombarded by parasitic interests, both internally and externally, that threaten to compromise the reason for their existence. I firmly believe we must rely upon our individual actions on the home front. In other words, after you depart Nahanni you will likely be filled with a new or renewed respect for nature. Don't let it slip away. Hold it near to your heart with all your will. Use it to give you a sense of purpose, a determination to protect your own natural environment.

With that thought, I'd like to leave you with a few words from my dear friend, Debbie Ladouceur (see page 10), and, oh yes, enjoy paddling your river of dreams.

Peter Jowett, July 1993

Using this Book

This book is intended to provide paddlers with all the information they need to enjoy the South Nahanni River to its fullest. To accomplish this the guide is organized into five parts.

"Before You Leave" supplies the necessary logistics for planning the trip and getting to and from the river.

"River Description" guides you down the river, indicating points of interest and suggesting some of the places you can hike to as side trips. In this edition a section of the Flat River within the park has been included as an alternative paddle to the more popular South Nahanni.

"River Maps" for the South Nahanni and Flat rivers are cross-referenced with the text through the use of bracketed numbers e.g. [64]. Bracketed numbers with an asterisk e.g [73*] indicate the position is approximate.

"The Nahanni Story" provides an interpretation of Nahanni's natural and human history. Again, points of interest are cross-referenced through the use of bracketed numbers which appear in the river description, on the maps, and in the Indices.

"Indices" include a quick reference to points of interest, a list of references, a guide to place names and a thorough index.

The Maps

The maps consist of 1:250,000 topographics enlarged to a scale of 1:125,000. While the enlargement assists with reading, they don't necessarily provide the detail needed to navigate river rapids or route-find while hiking. For these purposes you may wish to rely upon 1:50,000 topos.

Maps in the book are contiguous and should be read from the *bottom to the top* of the page, in the direction of travel. Arrows indicate the direction of river flow.

Note the *north sign varies slightly* with each map.

Black triangles indicate designated campgrounds; white triangles popular camping spots.

If you have any comments or information that could be used to update this book please feel free to write me care of the publisher:

Rocky Mountain Books
#4 Spruce Centre SW
Calgary, Alberta
Canada T3C 3B3

River Ratings

The following rapid-rating system was adopted for this description. Always bear in mind your remote location, the temperature of the water, and the consequences of losing gear.

Class I   • fast-moving water with riffles and small waves
   • clear routes
   • risk to swimmers is slight
   • self resue is easy

Class II   • straightforward rapids, possibly with low ledges, sweepers, large protruding boulders
   • Occasional maneuvering required
   • open boats may ship some water
   • clear channels are evident
   • Swimmers are seldom injured and group assistance is seldom needed

Class III   • rapids with moderate irregular waves which may be difficult to avoid. High irregular rocks, definite ledges, strong eddies and currents
   • large waves or strainers may be present but are easily avoided
   • route obstructed, requiring precise manoeuvring
   • open boats can be swamped
   • Swimmers are seldom injured, but group assistance may be required to avoid long swims
   • Scouting is advisable for inexperienced parties

Class IV   • Powerful rapids with large waves, lots of rocks, holes and boiling eddies
   • route obstructed, requiring fast precise manoeuvring under pressure
   • paddlers should have a strong eskimo roll
   • risk of injury to swimmers. Group assistance is often essential
   • Scouting is advisable the first time down

Note: Class III+ would be close to a Class IV, Class III++ is even closer. Class I rapids, although having tricky currents at times (such as where a large stream enters the river) are not shown on the accompanying maps.

I have basked in the light of many moons in Nahanni. I have felt the awe of her power flow through my veins. There are not many rivers left that can fill us with awe or demand our respect and humble us — the Nahanni is one.

The mystery and magic of the Nahanni River is felt with her every turn, each canyon, every rocky crag. The flat water of the Moose Ponds gives way to the boulder gardens where the Nahanni rages white with the coming of spring, then abruptly transforms into a wide, powerful, and deep river to Virginia Falls. From here, immense canyons dwarf those lucky enough to experience them. A sense of timelessness seeps into your bones — the feeling of a wisdom from these Rockies that transcends the ice ages, millions of years of birth and death. These are the wild places, a place of magic that man must not tear asunder. Let this magic heal your heart, soul, body, and mind.

Peter has left me the task of instilling you with the awareness and responsibility of protecting, respecting, and honouring the sacred land of the Nahanni. Be assured that each footstep and paddle stroke Peter has made throughout this vast land was with awe and respect. Follow his example — be responsible, have only honourable intentions for the land and yourself and you too will reap the benefits of the highest integrity.

As I left the Nahanni I looked back to the canyon system fading from view in a blood-red sunset. I questioned leaving the land of mystery, of magic and wonder, knowing that the plains would lead me back to the world of man. I do not worry, for one day I will return.

Debbie Ladouceur

Before You Leave

Slower going near Rabbitkettle. Hal Morrison at the end of the Moose Ponds trip described on page 53.

Previous pages: Rabbitkettle Lake at sunset, and the peaks of the Ragged Ranges.

Planning Your Trip

Congratulations, you've decided to embark on the trip of a lifetime. The first decision to make is where on the river to start your trip. There are several variables to consider, including expense, desired trip length, your party's paddling ability, the season and water levels.

Where to Start from and the Cost

The cheapest way to travel the South Nahanni is to follow in the path of the early pioneers: that is, track and paddle your canoe *up* river. I know of one solo paddler who tried this during moderate water levels in July. He ended up having an accident at the top of The Splits, lost most of his gear, nearly poked out his eye, and needed a ride off the river. It can be done, though. Neil Hartling of Nahanni River Adventures, along with friends and guides, tracked and paddled a Voyageur canoe, at low water levels, all the way up to Virginia Falls. Personally, this type of trip sounds pretty masochistic — not my idea of a holiday at all.

A less punishing but cheap option involves paddling down the Little Nahanni River (5-6 days) which offers some very challenging sections of whitewater to be attempted only by expert whitewater canoeists. The put in point is Flat Lakes at the end of Highway 10 past the Tungsten turn-off. Another option is the Flat River (5-8 days) reached near the Tungsten mining camp (which may still be closed) off Highway 10. People have had success going both ways. However, the Tungsten road is deteriorating and is currently impassable. You should phone the Yukon Department of Highways (403) 667-5322 for an update on conditions. Keep in mind that these options provides an additional challenge — retrieving your vehicle. You need two vehicles. If you can afford it, there is the option of drivers returning by float plane from Blackstone or Lindberg Landing. Tungsten mining camp has a wheeled aircraft landing strip.

Good friends of mine, Debbie Ladouceur and Dave Salayka, took yet another route. These intrepid souls drove 240 kilometres up Canol Road during the spring, then sledded their canoe and gear 80 kilometres over the continental divide to Moose Ponds. In total, they trudged 560 kilometres by snowshoe. As of 1987, their sled still stood upright on river left a few kilometres below Moose Ponds. The trip back to their vehicle was equally exciting and culminated in marriage at Ross River! In summer you can use the same access by descending the South MacMillan River from the Canol Road to Witham Creek. Ascend to Willow Lake, portage to the Ross River, ascend the Ross and portage to the Moose Ponds — a week of hard work. Read the Canadian Geographical Journal February/March 1977 for an account of this trip.

If chartering your own aircraft, the most economical method is to drive to your finishing point, either Blackstone Territorial Park or Lindberg Landing, and fly from there. But no matter what type of aircraft, or who you fly with, or where you fly from, it is going to cost you over one thousand dollars to get to Rabbitkettle Lake, and more to fly further upriver. To cut costs, you might consider sharing a charter with other parties. For example, if Simpson Air is using a Twin Otter, which has a very large capacity, it may be possible to split the charter cost between two or more parties.

Trip Length

For a fairly leisurely trip, most paddlers start from Rabbitkettle Lake and end at Blackstone Landing, a journey of about 12/13 days. Starting at Rabbitkettle Lake, one possible itinerary may look something like this:

Day 1	fly in by morning, organize gear, set up camp, hike to Rabbitkettle Hotsprings.
Day 2	portage to river, paddle to Flood Creek.
Day 3/4	paddle to Virginia Falls, set up camp, hike around the falls.
Day 5	hike Sunblood Mountain or Marengo Creek.
Day 6	portage to Fourth Canyon, paddle through the canyon and Figure 8 rapid, camp at Flat River confluence.
Day 7	paddle to The Gate, hike to Pulpit Rock overlook.
Day 8	paddle to Big Bend, hike up creek in the bend.
Day 9	paddle to Deadmen Valley with a stop to hike up Scow Creek.
Day 10	hike in Deadmen Valley area.
Day 11	paddle to Kraus Hotsprings, soak and camp, or camp at the top of The Splits.
Day 12/13	paddle to Nahanni Butte, de-register, paddle on to Blackstone Landing.

If you start at Island Lake add another two or three days, and another three or four days if you start from Moose Ponds. Allow five to eight days if descending the Little Nahanni or Flat Rivers. Add on several more days for rest days or bad weather days. Trip lengths vary depending on the time spent each day paddling, the amount of hiking you do, river speed and bad weather. Headwinds can slow you down dramatically.

Commercial River Outfitters

Many of Nahanni's visitors opt to travel with a river outfitter. Outfitters will supply most of your equipment, provide excellent meals, and employ experienced river guides to assist paddlers. I have dealt with most of the companies listed below and all offer excellent, safe, and worry-free adventure.

Nahanni River Adventures
Neil Hartling
Box 4869 Whitehorse, Yukon, Y1A 4N6
(403) 668-3180, fax (403) 668-3056
My friend, "Nahanni Neil," provides an excellent service for his clients, using good equipment and professional, friendly guides. This company also offers canoe and raft rentals.

Black Feather Wilderness Adventures
1341 Wellington St. W, Ottawa, Ontario, Department NR, K1Y 3B8
(613) 722-9717, fax (613) 722-0245

Nahanni Wilderness Adventures
Dave Hibbard
Box 4, Site 6, RR#1, Didsbury, Alberta, T0M 0W0
(403) 637-3843, fax (403) 637-3843

Whitewolf
2565 West 2nd Ave, Vancouver, BC, V6K 1J7
(604) 736-0664, fax (604) 736-2810

These companies, including Simpson Air which runs Nahanni Mountain Lodge at Little Doctor Lake, form the Nahanni River Outfitters Association (NROA). This association is responsible for maintaining professional levels of service and for fostering good operating ethics amongst outfitters in order to keep the South Nahanni River a beautiful and unspoiled place. To assist with this the NROA has established the Nahanni Trust Fund and requests that paddlers donate $1/day/person to assist programs and projects involving the local area and native community that are not already funded by other means. Donations are payable at either the park office or at the Nahanni-Ram Visitor Centre in Fort Simpson. Neil Hartling is the president of NROA, and you may address any questions and comments to him care of Nahanni River Adventures.

Registration

All travellers to Nahanni must register with park officials. This registration system serves several purposes. It allows park officials to pass on information to each paddler and helps keep track of the amount of traffic on the river. Most importantly, it alerts park wardens of the need for possible emergency assistance if a party is overdue. Without this safeguard, injured or lost persons would have to rely on discovery by aircraft or other paddlers. It's cheap insurance.

Although Park officials prefer you to register at the park office in Fort Simpson, you may also register with the park warden at Rabbitkettle Lake. (For those of you travelling the Flat River you don't have this option.) You must register either in person or by phoning the park office at (403) 695-3151. Remember, it is mandatory to de-register at the end of the trip and this must be done in person at one of three places; the office in Nahanni Butte village, at Fort Simpson or at Blackstone Landing or by phoning Fort Simpson collect. Please do not abuse this system. Ensure that you use the check-in stations located on the portage trail to Rabbitkettle Lake at the river, Virginia Falls campground, Deadmen Valley at the old forestry patrol cabin, and Kraus Hotsprings. The principle is simple. If, for example, an overdue party has signed in at Virginia Falls but not at Deadmen Valley, rescuers will then concentrate on the area between the two check-in stations rather than starting at the Broken Skull River or wherever. In other words, it reduces the area to be searched and speeds up rescue.

If you are starting the river above Rabbitkettle, keep in mind there are large stretches of hazardous river to navigate before you reach the park. In this case, I suggest you register with the RCMP at Fort Simpson or with a detachment nearest your starting point, or with a responsible friend or family member. It is important to give an estimated arrival date at Rabittkettle Lake. This will help protect you in case of an accident before you reach the park.

More Information

For more information about the park and its regulations write: Park Superintendent, Nahanni National Park, Postal Bag 300, Fort Simpson, NWT, X0E 0N0. Tel: 403-695-3151. Tourism information for the Northwest Territories is available at 1-800-661-0788, or by writing Travel Arctic, Economic and Development, Box 1320, Yellowknife, NWT, X1A 2L9.

When to Go — Weather and Seasons

The third week of July to the second week of August is the busiest part of the season and some places such as Virginia Falls can be very crowded. River outfitters have addressed this problem amongst themselves by staggering their trips, while park wardens have brought in new regulations restricting the size of groups to 12 persons. If you would like a little more solitude, paddle the river in late spring or early fall.

To help you decide when to go consider the following:

Geographic Location

Two significant geographic factors strongly influence the weather in this region. First, Nahanni's location in sub-arctic latitudes creates clearly defined seasons, the estimated amount of sunshine varying from 0.95 hours/day in December to 9.35 hours/day in June.

Duration of Daylight for Nahanni Region

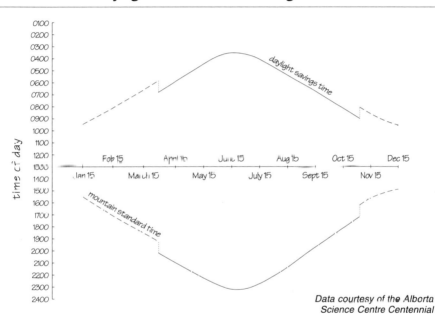

Data courtesy of the Alberta
Science Centre Centennial

The second factor is the mountain and canyon topography which affects temperature, precipitation, humidity, sunlight, and the surface flow of winds. Most river travellers understand the significance of high winds periodically experienced in canyons and valleys. In these areas airflow can become compressed, increasing in speed as it negotiates around obstacles. Mountainous topography causes cool air to drain from higher elevations into valley bottoms during the night, providing campers with an extra morning chill.

Sporadic and localized heavy rainfalls are also characteristic of mountain terrain. Once, while I was camping half a kilometre above the mouth of the Mary River and receiving only a drizzle of rain, campers at the river mouth experienced high winds and heavy rain for the entire night. The area where they had camped is exposed to westerly storms tracking into Third Canyon along the Mary River valley. If the weather looks a little questionable it might be wise not to set up camp where larger valleys join the South Nahanni.

Temperatures

Continental air masses create wide variations between winter and summer average temperatures. As measured at Fort Simpson, January is the coldest month with an average of -28.2°C, while July is the hottest with an average of 16.6°C. The monthly average temperatures for Fort Simpson (representative of the Mackenzie Plains) and Tungsten (representative of the Mackenzie Mountains) give a good indication of what Nahanni travellers can expect. Remember, these are average temperatures. In summer you can expect some hot days with afternoon temperatures hitting 30°C.

Average temperatures for Fort Simpson and Tungsten

	Fort Simpson	Tungsten
January	-28.3	-24.4
February	-22.8	-19.0
March	-14.9	-14.0
April	-2.5	-6.0
May	7.9	2.1
June	14.4	9.0
July	16.6	10.9
August	14.4	9.5
September	7.3	3.3
October	-1.9	-4.4
November	-15.6	-14.8
December	-24.5	-20.5
Annual	-4.2	-5.7

Rain and Snow

In summer, the moisture-laden continental storm track shifts to the north with the result that July and August are the wettest months of the year, recording 60 to 90 mm of precipitation per month. February and March are the driest with 15 to 30 mm per month. Rainfall in the area is mainly convective, resulting in evening and afternoon showers and thundershowers.

Most people associate the northern parts of Canada with cold and lots of snow. While Nahanni's winter is marked by cold dry Arctic air masses which bring cold temperatures, large snowfalls are not common. In fact, maximum snow depth varies from a mere 150 cm at low elevations to 200 cm in higher valleys. Because of the area's northerly location, however, accumulated snow often remains on the ground from October to mid-May at lower elevations and from September to June at higher elevations. Snow can fall at any time, even in summer, so be prepared for unseasonably cold temperatures.

Summer Storms and Water Levels

The South Nahanni River relies on the spring thaw and spring and summer rains to keep it charged. Seventy-six percent of its yearly discharge occurs from May to August, with peak flow occurring in June. Between May and the end of September you can expect to encounter, on average, 10 thunderstorms. During the peak visitation period of July and August heavy rainfalls associated with summer thunderstorms are relatively common and can dump as much as 90 mm of rain in 24 hours. This dramatically affects river water levels, flooding some of the more constricted valleys and posing a serious threat to hikers who should be wary of flash floods during or shortly after such storms. Changes in water level can alter the degree of difficulty of some river sections, especially rapids. Rarely does flooding actually cause the rivers to overfill their banks, but if there was a heavy snowfall the preceding winter the water table will remain high and the river will be more susceptible to storm floods.

Monthly Precipitation Normals (1951-1980)

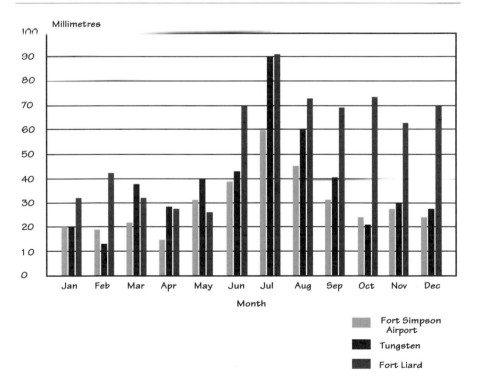

Wind

Winds generally blow from the west. Intensity and direction, as mentioned previously, are largely affected by the local topography. Valleys with an east-west orientation generally experience stronger winds than valleys perpendicular to the prevailing wind. When wind funnels down a canyon or valley, maximum speeds are reached at constrictions, such as sharp bends, where the wind is compressed. Be careful in these locations. Strong winds not only reduce canoe stability, they can also create large waves when the wind blows against the current.

Obviously, winds affect commercial air travel as well. I vividly recall flying over Yohin Ridge on one occasion and encountering a wind sheer which pulled us into a free fall from 3500 feet to 1500 feet in a matter of seconds. Only the skill of the pilot prevented us from being splattered into the ground. Fear not — have faith in your pilot!

River Freeze-up and Break-up

For those of you wishing to paddle the South Nahanni early or late in the season, the earliest recorded freeze-up occurred on October 23, 1962, while the latest occurred on November 30, 1958. On average you can expect freeze-up to occur around the 12th of November.

The earliest recorded break-up occurred on April 15, 1923, and the latest on May 19, 1961, giving an average of May 5th. Closer to the continental divide, freeze-up will naturally occur earlier and break-up later.

If you plan to continue on to the Liard and Mackenzie Rivers be aware that the South Nahanni is a much smaller river and is subject to freezing and break-up earlier than the other two.

Average dates for river freeze-up and break-up

	Rabbitkettle Hotsprings to Virginia Falls	Virginia Falls to Deadmen Valley	Deadmen Valley to Nahanni Butte
mean elevation (m.a.s.l.)	600	400	250
formation of first permanent ice	October 18	October 20	October 21
complete freeze-up	November 12	November 14	November 14
first deterioration of ice	May 6	May 3	May 1
water clear of ice	May 9	May 6	May 4

What to Bring

Organization is the key to a successful trip. I have included a list of equipment, organized in a manner that helps prevent me from forgetting anything, that has proven useful on some of my longer 900 kilometres or more northern canoe trips.

Personal Gear

- running shoes for around camp
- lightweight hiking boots
- several pairs of wool socks
- one set of polypropylene long underwear
- two pairs of lightweight nylon pants
- two pairs of heavy bush pants
- rain pants
- underwear
- two pairs of shorts, one to double as a swim suit
- T-shirts
- one light, long-sleeved shirt and one heavier shirt ideally made of a wool blend
- wool sweater
- pile jacket
- rain jacket and pants
- anorak with hood
- sun hat and wool toque
- bandana
- toiletries, including a good waterproof suncream
- book and guide books
- notebook and pencil
- insect repellent
- bear repellent
- camera gear and film
- sunglasses
- glasses strap

All of this is stored in a medium-gauge plastic bag sealed with a heavy twist tie (garbage bags are too thin to last long) and placed in a waterproof pack. If possible use the modern canoeist's drybags.

Paddling Gear

Personal Equipment
- wet boots
- wet suit (Farmer John style)
- knee pads
- paddling gloves
- fanny pack for emergency gear mentioned on page 23
- life jacket with knife and whistle attached
- paddle jacket

Group Gear

- canoe with yoke and floating painters held onto the bow and stern caps in a coil with an elasticized cord. Across the length of the thwart closest to the stern I stretch an elasticized cord which I use to hold down a map. Under the bowcap I suspend a mini hammock where the bow person can place a hat, sunglasses etc. when not involved in whitewater. I have drilled holes at strategic spots in the gunnels along the cargo section of the canoe and tied small loops of cord through them. These serve as anchor spots for tying in packs etc.
- spray skirt with rigging for an extra paddle and easy entry ports
- two paddles plus a spare
- sponge and plastic bailing can with cord to loop around a thwart
- two pieces of five-millimetre nylon sling rope, approximately four to five metres long, used to tie-in gear
- a half-inch thick, roughly 76 cm x 76 cm piece of plywood tapered to fit the inside bottom contour of the canoe from the yoke to the seat. By piling gear on this platform, it is kept out of any water that collects in the bottom of the canoe. To add support and to allow water underneath, attach two strips of wood along the length of the platform underside. Hinges and holes for handles can be added for portability. Add duct tape to the platform edges to protect the inside of the canoe. This platform also works quite well as a kitchen table.
- two waterproof packs and two waterproof barrels. I use an old internal-frame pack to protect one waterproof pack from abrasions/punctures and a home-made protector for the other. I have adapted the internal-frame pack to carry the barrels on portages. It also functions as a day pack with the use of compression straps.
- throw bags

Camping Gear

- self-supporting tent with fly and mosquito net. I treat the non-breathing parts of the tent and fly with a couple of coats of waterproofing paint-on silicone.
- plastic ground sheet
- three-season down sleeping bags packed in medium-gauge plastic bags (not garbage bags) sealed with heavy twist ties and stored in compression sacks. These are then placed in the waterproof packs. I've had lots of dumps and but never a wet, cold sleep using this packing method.
- Therm-A-Rests stored the same way as sleeping bags

Cooking Gear

- backpack stove and fuel stored in fuel bottles with pour spout
- waterproof matches or matches dipped in wax, and butane lighters
- stainless steel nested cookset and small grill
- utensils, plates, cups, and bowls
- water bottles with graduations on sides for measuring liquids
- food, spices, etc. Label breakfasts, lunches, and suppers in separate bags
- biodegradable dish soap, pot scrubber, dish cloth
- large pot with spout and bail handle for washing-up which can also be used to heat water for portable showers
- heavy-gauge plastic bag for garbage

Emergency Gear

- flagging tape
- small flare kit and bear bangers
- emergency locator device
- reflector blanket
- two 7 mm slings, 3-5 metres long
- three carabiners
- two rescue pulleys
- waterproof matches
- extra knife
- insect repellent
- high energy food bars
- basic first aid supplies

I carry this equipment in a fanny pack which I wear while paddling hazardous stretches. At night I leave the fanny pack attached to the canoe seat in case I have to exit camp quickly due to a bear attack etc. I also leave the life jackets paddles and throw bags in the canoe.

Repair Gear

- sewing awl and waxed thread for clothing, tent, and packs
- extra tent pole and pegs, nylon repair tape
- matches dipped in wax, and butane lighters
- canoe-repair kit
- people-repair kit. A good all-round first-aid kit can usually be stored together with the other repair kit in one organized kit with pouches.
- duct tape

Miscellaneous Gear

- headlamps
- portable shower bag
- folding saw and hatchet
- polyethylene tarp with several four to fiver-metre pieces of nylon cord already tied on for quick use
- extra rope/nylon sling for clothes line etc.
- maps and good compass

Raft and Canoe Rentals

Paddlers from outside the US and Canada should be aware that canoes can be rented locally:

- Deh Cho Sports, Box 280, Fort Simpson, NWT, X0E 0N0. (403) 695-2320, fax (403) 695-2147
- North Nahanni Expediting and Transit Tours, Box 254, Fort Simpson, NWT, X0E 0N0. (403) 695-3601
- Simpson Air, Box 260, Fort Simpson, NWT, X0E 0N0. (403) 695-2505, Fax (403) 695-2925
- Liard Tours Limited, Box 3190, Fort Sipmson, BC, V0C 1R0. (604) 774-2909 Fax (604) 774-2908

Maps

Maps in this book are 1:250,000 topographics that have been doubled in size to give a scale of 1:125,000 (1 inch = 2.5 miles). These maps are not intended to replace regular topographic maps. If you are looking for precise information you should purchase the appropriately scaled 1:50,000 topos.

These are the 1:250,000 (1 inch = 5 miles) topographic maps you will need to paddle from Moose Ponds to Blackstone Landing:

Little Nahanni River 105 I: from Moose Ponds to just downstream of Moore's Hotspring, it includes the Little Nahanni River.

Glacier Lake 95 L: from just passed Moore's Hotspring to the top of the park.

Flat River 95 E: from the top of the park to above Sunblood, it includes most of the Flat River.

Virginia Falls 95 F: from Sunblood to Kraus Hotsprings, it includes the rest of the Flat River.

Sibbeston Lake 95 G: from The Splits to just short of Blackstone Landing.

Frances Lake 105 H: for the headwaters of the Flat River.

For additional detail, perhaps to have a good look at contour lines for hiking, 1:50,000 (1 inch = 1 mile) topo maps are also available.

For the rapids located below Moose Ponds, you will need the following 1:50,000 topo maps:

105 I/13 Mount Wilson

105 I/14 Jones Lake

105 I/11

105 I/10

105 I/7 Dozer Lake

105 I/8 Mount Appler

95 L/5 Black Wolf Mountain

95 L/4 Mount Sir Douglas MacBrien

95 L/3 Dolf Mountain

95 E/14 Hole-in-the-Wall Lake

For a complete list and to purchase maps contact:
    Energy Mines and Resources Canada
    Cartographic Information and Distribution Centre
    615 Booth Street, Ottawa, Ontario, K1A 0E9

Getting There & Back

Before the real adventure can begin a great deal of preparation is required, including determining how to get to the river. There are a few options, but with no direct road or motorized-watercraft access allowed in the park most people choose to fly in. If you go this route, try to pick an air-charter company that best suits your needs as far as timing, cost, and drop-off point are concerned. See page 13 for non-flying options to the South Nahanni River outside the park.

Where to fly in to

- *Moose Ponds* Before deciding to start here, take careful note of the water level downstream — the amount of spring run-off and summer rain significantly affects water levels for this section. During spring runoff this is a very serious piece of water, requiring advanced paddling skills. Overall, I would rate it as class III+ to IV at this time of year. On the other hand, by the end of July the water level can be too low to float some sections of rapids. Current daily water levels are available from the park office after 1:30 pm each day.

- *Island Lake* This lake is located so close to the river, it requires only two brief portages. Before you land, have a look at Haywire Lake and Honeymoon Lake. Depending on the weather and size of the plane, landing at these lakes may allow you to paddle to the river instead of portaging. Ask your pilot.

- *Gravel bar above Brintnell Creek* This is the only spot in Nahanni where you can land a plane on wheels. It is very dependent on water levels and is not an option during spring flooding. The position indicated on the map is approximate.

- *Rabbitkettle Lake* Float planes of all sizes can land here. There is a campground and warden cabin, and the portage to the river is an easy half-kilometre.

- *Virginia Falls* You can use this as the starting point for a shorter trip. Landing here is an option at all water levels. The plane drops you off at the campground.
- *Seaplane Lake* This spot is used to paddle a short section of the Flat River should you wish to join the South Nahanni below Virginia Falls. So that you don't miss out on Nahanni's greatest attraction, the wardens are considering cutting a hiking trail from the Flat River to Virginia Falls.
- *Flat Lakes* The starting point for the Little Nahanni River route to the South Nahanni which is joined north of Island Lake.

Air-charter Companies

As of 1993 there are six air-charter companies to choose from:

- *Simpson Air* is the largest of the companies flying charters into Nahanni. It is owned and operated by Ted Grant who has served as an unofficial ambassador for Fort Simpson and Nahanni for several years, promoting tourism and bringing Nahanni to the world stage. Ted offers an excellent service using a variety of aircraft including Cessna 185's, a 206 and 207, and Twin Otters. You had best check to see which aircraft are being used for the South Nahanni River. Simpson Air also rents canoes and rafts. The address is Box 260, Fort Simpson, NWT, X0E 0N0. (403) 695-2505, fax (403) 695-2925.
- *Watson Lake Flying Services* flies a single engine Otter, a piston Beaver, and a 185 and 205 Cessna from Watson Lake. The address is Box 7, Watson Lake, Yukon Territory, Y0A 1C0. (403) 536-2231 or fax (403) 536-2399.
- *Liard Tours Limited* is operated by Urs and Marianne Schildknecht. I've flown with Urs on several occasions and he is an excellent pilot. Liard Tours flies a piston Beaver from Fort Nelson and can carry three passengers with gear and a canoe strapped to the floats. It also offers a shuttle service back to Fort Nelson and a canoe rental service. The address is Box 3190, Fort Nelson, BC, V0C 1R0. (604) 774-2909, fax (604) 774-2908.
- *Blackstone Aviation,* owned by Paul and Margret Jones, operates a 185 Cessna from Lindberg Landing near the Blackstone Territorial Park. The advantage of flying from here is that you can paddle back to your vehicle without incurring additional shuttle or travel costs, or taking extra time. The only problem is the limited capacity of the 185 Cessna, which can only carry 300 kilograms plus pilot and a canoe tied onto the floats. With careful planning and packing, this is the most efficient way for a party of two to get upriver. The address is Box 117, Fort Simpson, NWT, X0E 0N0. (403) 695-2111, fax (403) 695-2132, or via the mobile telephone operator – Arrowhead Channel YJ39704.

- *Deh Cho Air* flies from Fort Liard with a piston Beaver and possibly a 185 Cessna. It also offers a canoe rental service. Contact c/o Liard Band Development Corporation, General Delivery, Fort Liard, NWT, X0E 0A0. (403) 770-4103.

- *Wolverine Air* is owned by Chris Pinckard and flies Cessna 206 and 185 aircraft. Wolverine Air flies out of Fort Simpson and the address is Box 316, Fort Simpson, NWT, X0E 0N0. (403) 695-2263, fax (403) 695-3400.

In brief, your choices are to fly from either Fort Nelson, Fort Liard, Lindberg Landing, Fort Simpson, or Watson Lake.

In case you are quoted a price based on air mileage, here are some distances in statute miles (the measure used by air charter companies) to help you out:

Fort Simpson to   Glacier Lake, 204
Rabbitkettle Lake, 194
Seaplane Lake, 185
Virginia Falls, 147
Nahanni Butte, 90
Blackstone Landing, 72

Now you have decided where to begin your adventure and have chosen an air-charter company (if you are using one), the next step is getting to the air-charter company base.

By Air to the Northwest Territories

If you are flying into Canada from the US or from overseas, you will most likely arrive at Vancouver (British Columbia), or Calgary or Edmonton (Alberta).

From these cities as well as from other parts of Canada, Air Canada and Canadian Airlines both fly to Yellowknife, Northwest Territories. From Yellowknife, NWT Air flies a regularly scheduled service to Fort Simpson. If coming from Vancouver, the most direct flight is via Whitehorse in the Yukon. Canadian Airlines also flies to Fort Nelson, British Columbia.

As you will have read, a number of air charter companies fly out of both Fort Simpson and Fort Nelson.

By Road to the Northwest Territories

Assuming you are travelling by road, there are two possible routes to follow. Whichever route you choose, expect two long days driving from major centres of population.

The Alaska Highway (Hwy. 97), accessible from Calgary/Edmonton, Vancouver, Prince George, Whitehorse and Fairbanks, accesses Fort Nelson and Watson Lake. The highway is paved and easy to drive. To get to Fort Liard, Blackstone Landing and Fort Simpson, turn off just west of Fort Nelson and take the Liard Highway (#77 in BC, #7 in NWT). Although a good, four-season, gravel road, it can be quite rough driving, so bring an extra headlight or two and a dependable spare tire.

The Mackenzie Highway (Hwy. 1) is an alternative route to Fort Simpson and Blackstone Landing if you are coming from Yellowknife, Hay River and northern Alberta. The paved section ends at the Fort Providence turn-off. From here the highway is a good four-season gravel road. A free ferry service takes vehicles across the Liard River to Fort Simpson, another 63 km distant. To avoid arriving after the ferry has stopped running for the day phone 1-800-661-0751 for the schedule.

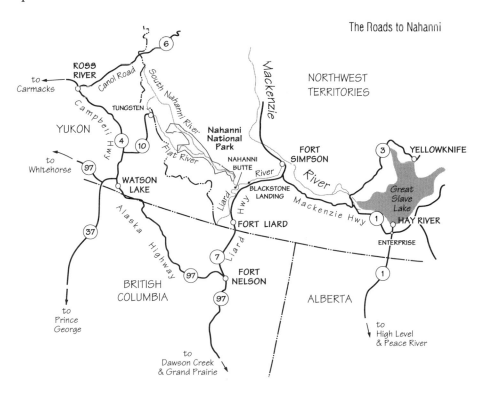

The Roads to Nahanni

Available services

The following gives you an idea of what services are available in some of the northern towns as you pass through:

- *Watson Lake, Yukon* offers full services, including gas, mechanical work, food, lodging, campgrounds and RCMP detachment (403-536-5555).
- *Ross River, Yukon* offers full services including gas, mechanical work, food, lodging, campgrounds and RCMP detachment (403-969-5555 or 667-5555).
- *Fort Nelson, BC* is the largest town along the Alaska Highway on the way to Nahanni from the south. It has full services, including an RCMP detachment (604-774-2777) and a hospital with an ambulance service (emergency 604- 774-6916). You will need to gas-up here for the 175 kilometre drive to Fort Liard, and to take extra **gas** with you. On one occasion when I drove through Fort Liard during the day the gas station was closed and it's another 280 kilometres to Fort Simpson!
- *Fort Liard, NWT* is a small village with a population of about 400 people. Services are limited: a gas station which may be closed, accommodations, food, and an RCMP detachment (403-770-4221). The natives from this village are famous for their birch-bark baskets, moose-hair tuftings, and beautiful moccasins.
- *Fort Simpson, NWT* has a population of about one thousand people and is fully serviced with a garage, Hudson Bay store, accommodations, restaurants, and a campground. There is an RCMP detachment (403-695-3111) and a hospital (403-695-2291). The park headquarters (403-695-3151) is located here.
- *Yellowknife NWT* is a small city on the shores of Great Slave Lake and offers visitors a complete range of services and tourist attractions. RCMP 403-920-8314, Hospital 403-920-4111.
- *Hay River NWT* offers full services, including gas, mechanical work, food and lodging. RCMP 403-874-6555, Hospital 403-874-6512.
- *Enterprise NWT* has a gas station and restaurant. This is the last gas station before Fort Simpson on the Mackenzie Highway, so top up the tank. RCMP 403-874-5555.

Recommended Travel Books and Maps:

The Milepost, All-the-North Travel Guide Alaska Northwest Publishing Company, updated regularly.

Explorer's Map Available free from Travel Arctic, Government of the Northwest Territories, Yellowknife, NWT, Canada X1A 2L9.

Leaving Nahanni

All river travellers must de-register from the park at one of the following locations; Nahanni Butte (a small native village), at the park office in Fort Simpson, or at Blackstone Landing visitor centre. Nahanni Butte village has an airstrip for wheeled aircraft, an emergency radiotelephone, a part-time nursing station, and a general store that is occasionally open. There is also a spot for camping. The village is only accessible by vehicle during the winter months.

Blackstone Landing, which is where most paddlers end their trip, is roughly another six-hour paddle from Nahanni Butte depending on river conditions. Here at Blackstone Territorial Park the NWT government provides a campground, drinking water, docking facilities for float planes and boats, and an emergency radio telephone. You can also purchase films and videos.

From here, a Fort Simpson taxi service offers a pick up service for paddlers and gear wishing to return to Fort Simpson. Phone North Nahanni Expediting and Transit Tours, Box 254, Fort Simpson, NWT, X0E 0N0. (403) 695-3601 to make arrangements. Rates are reasonable. Presumably you can also arrange with the taxi service to take you further afield to Fort Liard, Fort Nelson, and Watson Lake should it be necessary.

Paddlers needing to return to their starting point at Flat Lakes (headwaters of the Little Nahanni) and having no second vehicle should make arrangements with Blackstone Aviation to return via float plane, with or without their gear which can be picked up later by car. It may be possible to reduce costs further by having one person share a flight (if space allows) with a party going in to Island Lake or the Moose Ponds. Reaching Tungsten — the put in point for the upper Flat River — is a little more difficult without that second car. It's suggested you take a float plane to Divide Lake, then walk. There is no air strip for wheeled aircraft at either Blackstone or Lindberg Landing.

Long-time residents Sue and Edwin Lindberg operate a bed and breakfast just upriver from Blackstone Landing at Lindburg Landing. Their place is also accessible by road. Although a shower and sauna are available, accommodation is quite rustic so you'll need your own sleeping bag, towel etc. For reservations phone the Fort Nelson Mobile Operator at JR36644 on the Arrowhead Channel. The Lindbergs are great folks, and I'm sure you'll enjoy a visit.

I've never paddled to Fort Simpson from Blackstone Landing but understand it takes about three to four days on generally slow water. There are two rapids along the way, the most serious being Beaverdam Rapids, located about 15 kilometres downstream of Poplar River. Here, a dangerous stopper wave extends two-thirds across the river. Keep to river right.

If at some point you find yourself with spare time in Fort Simpson you should visit the Fort Simpson Information Centre. The town itself operates the Nahanni-Ram Visitor Centre, also offering video and slide programs. You can take a boat trip on the Mackenzie River, an historical walking tour of the town (goes every evening), or visit a native friendship centre for a variety of activities. A golf course is scheduled to open in 1994 or 1995.

Travel Tips

In this section I am presenting safety tips and techniques which will help you travel safely, comfortably and with the minimum impact on the environment.

Paddling

Tracking and Lining Techniques

Tracking is the technique used for towing a canoe upstream. Two lines are used to control the canoe. A front line should be tied in the form of a bridle so that the pull is from the underside of the canoe, reducing the possibility of flipping. The second line is tied to a downstream thwart. Tracking is accomplished by letting the current hit the canoe at a slight angle, thereby holding the canoe out and away from the bank where you are walking. This angle is tricky to get right. Too much angle and the water broadsides the canoe, threatening to flip it. Too little and the canoe will just pull to shore. It takes a little practice but once you've mastered the technique it allows you to walk your canoe up routes like the Flat River or Prairie Creek.

Lining is the technique used for leading your canoe downstream. The technique is the same except the bridle must be attached to the upstream end of the canoe. The following two diagrams illustrate an easy and effective way of attaching a tracking or lining bridle to your canoe.

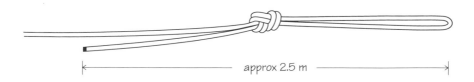

approx 2.5 m

Tie an overhand or figure 8 in the rope so that the loop and the loose end are approximately the same length

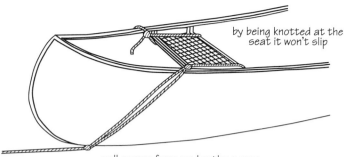

by being knotted at the seat it won't slip

pull comes from under the canoe

Tie the doubled portion of the rope around one end of the seat and the single rope around the other seat so that the knot is under the keel.

Safety Ideas

This is the paddling equipment I find particularly useful:

- 1/8-inch wet suit and wet boots. No matter what the air temperature, these should always be worn when paddling sections such as rapids where there is always the possibility of having to swim. If you do end up in the water, this thermal protection will allow you to function better and for longer. Without it, a person can begin to lose control of his or her limbs in four to five minutes. Paddling gloves are nice to have as well.
- life jacket with whistle and knife attached.
- properly outfitted throw bag.
- a spray skirt or some means to keep waves from spilling into the boat. A spray skirt also helps to keep you warm during rainy, windy days.

Throughout your paddling trip, and particularly when dealing with rapids, take extra care during flood conditions. The South Nahanni responds quickly to significant rainfall. For this same reason, when camping be sure to bring your canoe high up on shore and tie it, a practice that will also protect it from high winds common in the canyons and on the Prairie Creek fan.

If you are travelling with one canoe or in small groups you should consider grouping-up with other canoes when paddling rapids. The additional assistance may prove useful.

If you are paddling rapids or just fast-moving water in a remote setting where the chance of getting immediate assistance is slim, you should take an additional precaution. This entails carrying a few essentials in a fanny pack strapped around you while in the canoe. Years ago I purchased a very handy fanny pack that folds out into a day pack for short hikes. I can also recommend the Seal Line waterproof fanny pack from Cascade Designs, which is superb.

In your fanny pack, you should consider carrying:

- flagging tape
- small flare kit and bear bangers
- bear repellent
- emergency locator device
- small reflector blanket
- waterproof matches
- small extra knife
- insect repellent
- high-energy food bars
- basic first-aid supplies

Essentially, take everything you will need should you become separated from your canoe and supplies for a short time. In addition to this list, I like to carry two seven-mm slings, three carabiners and two rescue pulleys in case I end up with a pinned canoe. My floating painters and throw bag rope can act as the main haul line.

Swimming

The mean temperature of the South Nahanni lies between 10 and 15 degrees Celsius during July and August. However, an influx of rain can dramatically cool the water, even during the hot summer months. Needless to say, this water is too cool to enjoy a leisurely swim — unless you're an ex-chief park warden I know! Rabbitkettle Lake is usually much warmer. While at Rabbitkettle Lake take time to sit on the dock and dangle your feet in the water. Instantly, hordes of minnows will come and nibble on your feet and between your toes. The feeling is so neat it should be illegal! Joking aside, prolonged exposure to Nahanni's cold waters can induce hypothermia.

Fishing

Your best chance for successful fishing is in clearer water entering the river from tributary streams. Arctic grayling, Dolly Varden, Lake Trout, and Northern Pike are the primary game fish. You might wonder why the Canadian Parks Service allows recreational fishing to continue when its mandate requires the protection of all natural components of the park. Are fish less worthy of protection than a caribou or an aster? This may provide a night's campfire discussion.

To fish in the national park you require a national park fishing licence, currently available for $13 at any national park, at Fort Simpson, and from the warden at Rabbitkettle Lake. A licence is also required to fish outside the park. This costs Canadian residents $15 for a 3-day licence or $20 for the year. Non-residents must pay $30 for a 3-day pass or $40 for the year.

Hiking

The Nahanni offers some of the most scenic and exhilarating hiking you could possibly wish for. The majority of hikes don't follow man-made trails. Instead, routes follow dry stream beds, stream banks, alluvial fans, and exposed alpine ridges where there are less impediments to walking. To have as little impact as possible, use game or human trails and walk on rock wherever possible. Try to avoid wet and boggy areas where vegetation and soil are easily damaged. If you encounter wildlife, back off and give them right-of-way. After all, you are in their home! Weather can change very rapidly, so be prepared. In this neck of the woods, temperatures have been known to drop 15°C in a couple of hours.

Seventeen of Nahanni's more popular hikes are described briefly in the River Description section. Be advised that the mapped routes in this book are only approximations and you should really take along the appropriate 1,50,000 topo maps for longer and more complicated trips. Difficulty wise, the hikes range from very easy strolls on Prairie Creek fan to difficult hikes like the multi-day backpack onto Tlogotsho Plateau.

Camping with an Environmental Conscience

Camping Locations

The maps in the River Description section identify some of the more popular camping areas. In the park, designated campgrounds have at least one picnic table, a pit privy, a fireplace, and a food cache.

Be aware that at Rabbitkettle Lake you are required to use the designated campsite, unless you arrive from the river side, in which case you can overnight on the island across from Rabbitkettle landing. Likewise, if you plan to stay near Virginia Falls, you must use the designated campsite. You are not required to stay at any of the other designated campsites — Marengo Creek, The Gate, Big Bend, Deadmen Valley and Kraus Hotsprings.

Although park literature states that paddlers are not to camp at outfitter camps, this is no longer true; you are welcome to camp there if you wish. For the most part, these camps have been dismantled.

The true measure of success for ecologically sound camping comes when you leave and are unable to spot a trace, other than footprints, of your presence at the site. This is the perfect camp.

The following are suggestions for ecologically sound camping:

- Don't dig drainage ditches around your tent. Instead, pitch your tent on a slight incline if possible and use a ground sheet.
- Open areas are good places to set up. The additional breeze will help keep bugs away and allow you to have a better and safer view of your surroundings.
- Avoid camping in alpine areas where vegetation is sensitive to disturbance and the growing season is brief.
- Camping at creek mouths, on beaches, and on gravel bars does less damage to the soil, prevents erosion, and protects the vegetation. Evidence of human use will be washed away by the next period of high water.
- Don't cut vegetation to make a bed or shelter, unless your life depends on it.
- If possible, move your tent daily or lift it up to allow the light to hit any vegetation trapped under the floor.
- Please, don't make chairs, tables etc. from trees. Bring them with you if you must. There are several compact and lightweight versions available.

Fires

The Nahanni River Outfitters Association (NROA), in cooperation with the park, are now providing collapsible fire boxes for those of you who wish to use open fires. This is an attempt to reduce the number of unsightly and destructive fire scars often found in camping areas. The intense heat from a fire sterilizes the soil, prevents vegetation growth, and causes erosion. Park officials would prefer it if campers used only stoves, but they realize there are times when an open fire is necessary.

If you must use a fire, then consider the following suggestions:

- Use existing fire rings and, if a ring appears heavily used, leave it for others rather than dismantling it. This will reduce the number of new rings built.
- If you must create a new fire ring, make it small, close to water, away from overhanging branches, and on bare mineral soil so the fire won't burn underground. Destroy the ring before you leave by pitching the rocks into the water and dispersing the ashes in the water. If you had to clear the site down to the mineral soil, scatter some organic debris, such as dead leaves, grass, and small twigs over the site to encourage rotting and site rehabilitation. If the fire is built on a grassy area, dig up the sod to expose mineral soil, then replace the sod after you've cleaned out the pit before leaving. If the fire is built on bare rock, first spread a thin layer of soil over the rock to protect it from blackening. In Nahanni, it is very easy to find exposed silty soils to build a fire on.

- Only use dead, fallen wood for fuel. Often dead, standing trees provide homes for woodpeckers and other wildlife.

- Remember, your impact is not restricted just to the fire pit itself; the area surrounding the fire gets trampled as well, so choose your site carefully.

- Keep a careful eye on the fire, especially during high winds and very dry weather. Never leave a fire unsupervised until you are positive it is out. You should be able to handle the ashes before leaving.

- If you burn wood with a maximum diameter no greater than your wrist, it is more likely to burn away to white ash and leave less mess to clean up.

During late spring, summer, and early fall the threat of forest fires is very real. If you are using an open fire, try to determine the degree of dryness around you by snapping small sticks and by feeling the amount of dampness in the forest litter on the ground. This will give you an indication of potential fire hazard. Please be especially careful in high winds which can carry sparks long distances. Lightning strikes account for roughly three-quarters of all wildfires, so keep an eye out for smoke after lightning storms. Remember, it is your legal responsibility to report all wildfires to authorities such as park wardens.

Drinking Water

Consider three natural conditions before dipping your cup:

First, the Meilleur River contains unusually high levels of arsenic — don't drink this water.

Second, giardiasis or "beaver fever" is certainly not unknown in the park. The culprit is the *Giardia lamblia* parasite which enters the water through infected animal feces and loves nothing better than to ride along in your small intestine. To prevent infection you must boil your drinking water for at least five minutes or filter it through a water purifying filter. Don't rely on halizone or chlorine tablets; these chemicals won't kill the little beggers. Iodine is effective if given a long enough contact time and the temperature is higher than 10 degrees Celcius. Those who become infected will exhibit the following symptoms about 15 days after ingestion: weakness, loss of appetite, diarrhoea, abdominal cramps, soft yellowish, greasy-looking, foul-smelling feces, gas, and a bloated feeling.

Thirdly, the sulphur-laden water flowing from Moore's and Kraus Hotsprings is not drinkable.

As a general rule, before you choose a source of drinking water always look around the area for natural contaminants nearby including carcasses.

There is considerable silt (turbidity) in the South Nahanni and many of its tributaries, especially during spring run-off and after storms. This is the result of glacial silts that wash into the river and cause the hissing sound you hear against the bottom of your canoe. The load thins dramatically as winter approaches, and the waters become much clearer. This new clarity can scare the stuffing out of you! After a summer of navigating the park patrol jet-boat in murky waters it was quite disconcerting to actually see how little clearance between the hull and some rocks there really was! Throughout the spring, summer and early fall the silt is usually above 1,000 mg/l. Flood concentrations are likely to exceed 20,000 mg/l.

One hot, sunny day, while hiking along the Virginia Falls portage, I heard the strained and muttered curses that occasionally announce the approach of portages. I stepped aside and stared in disbelief as a number of overburdened souls passed by carrying several large, heavy containers of water! Apparently, they thought the silt in the river prevented them from drinking it. Since they had carried the water that far I didn't have the heart to tell them their efforts were unnecessary. Remaining silent and smiling widely, I turned and continued on my merry way!

Don't let this silty river water fool you. It's great! Just let it stand for a half hour or so until some of the silt has settled out. Less silty water is usually available from tributary streams such as Whitespray Spring which offers some of the best drinking water on the Nahanni. If you're still not convinced this water is safe, consider this: the same type of silt is used in coffee conditioners, the only difference being the addition of sweeteners and whiteners.

Unfortunately, even some of the high, remote alpine lakes, such as Hole-in-the-Wall, have traces of chemical pollutants. I guess this is a sign of the times when worldwide pollution can be found in even the most remote corners of the earth. This should give a person something to think about the next time he or she applies chemicals to the lawn in order to burn more gas by mowing it more often.

Human Waste

Although designated campgrounds have privies, most of the time you will have to find your own. In ideal conditions, an option is to dig a hole six to ten inches deep, removing the sod plug intact without removing the topsoil. Topsoil provides the bacterial action necessary to decompose feces. If the hole is to be used more than once, spread a thin layer of soil on the feces after each use. For a multi-use hole, dig the pit longer or wider rather than deeper.

Before leaving the site, lay the sod back in place. There should be a slight mound which will ultimately subside with decomposition. If a mound is absent, then a depression will form, collect water, and eventually erode. Make sure the whole site is located well away from any water, at least 100 metres. The feces will decompose quite quickly, but toilet paper will last a long time. I always burn the paper, poking it with a twig to ensure it all burns. If it is impossible to dig a hole, hike even further away from camp and do without the toilet paper.

Waste Water

If you have a campfire, slowly pour your waste water around the edge of the flame where it will burn away. If you don't have a fire, pour the water into your latrine hole. Food particles can attract unwelcome wildlife like bears, so dispose of them properly. Use biodegradable soap in small quantities.

When collecting water, use a container that will allow you to make only one or two trips. Continuous walking on vegetation will kill it and cause erosion, especially near water.

Please don't wash yourself or your dishes directly in the water source. I remember how I hated seeing someone washing themselves in Rabbitkettle Lake, the source of my drinking water. Haul some water and bathe away from the water source.

Garbage

It's simple: pack out what you pack in. If you brought in cans, burn and crush them to reduce bulk. Burn what you can and pack out everything else. This includes the foil that seems to be in most packaging these days.

Remember to cache the garbage with your food in an odour and bird-proof bag. Never bury garbage. Animals will dig it up, possibly causing themselves injury or, at the very least, making a hell of a mess. Dispose of fish guts by completely burning them in a hot fire or by leaving them in the moving water of a river or stream. Considering the limited number of visitors using the Nahanni, I can't foresee throwing the entrails into the river as having a large negative effect.

Wildlife Pests and Hazards

As you will read in the Fur, Feather, and Fins chapter, there is a wide variety of wildlife living in this part of the Territories. Undoubtedly, you will spend many great moments watching the numerous species interacting with each other and with their surroundings. Depending on your actions, these encounters can be safe and very enjoyable, providing memories and photographs that will last a lifetime. There are, however, limitations and sometimes travellers are hurt as a result of their own ignorance. For example, if a person was to poke his finger into a least weasel hole he could have the end bitten off, or if he was to approach too close to a doe's fawn he might get trampled.

On some occasions, however, circumstances will be beyond your control. It helps to keep in mind that all wildlife can be dangerous, especially when cornered and without an escape route, when protecting their young, or when in a feverish state during the mating season. For this reason it is prudent to travel with your head up and with a full awareness of your surroundings. This may help you avoid, for example, the wild-eyed and extremely dangerous bull moose in rut.

Bugs

During your trip on the South Nahanni you will undoubtedly become intimately involved with several of these pests. They are always horrendous from the end of The Splits to Blackstone Landing until after the first frosts arrive. I believe the last record number of mosquitos killed in a single slap at Nahanni Butte was 43! We used to joke that a person would surely die if he tripped while running to the park office from the river.

There are only two effective methods to contend with these critters: use plenty of bug repellent and/or wear clothing from head to toe, including a head net. The two types of bug jackets, impregnated and simple barrier, are quite effective. Tents **must** have a zippered bug screen with a reliable zipper. Generally, mosquitoes won't be too bothersome if you remain close to a smoky campfire. If you are in the north country for awhile, you will become so accustomed to their hum you will not be able to fall asleep without their familiar lullaby. Well, almost!

Bears

There are two species inhabiting Nahanni: the Black Bear and the Grizzly. Both can be extremely dangerous to humans. Although there are several preventative measures which lessen this risk, keep in mind there will always be an element of chance involved.

To date, the majority of bear encounters have been non-injurious; either the bear was not interested or, if it charged, it was only to scare the person off (quite effectively I might add!). These incidents are so uncommon it would be a shame for a person to miss the delights of the outdoors because of a fear of bears. Attacks resulting in any form of injury are very rare considering the number of people who make use of bear country.

Throughout my career and while travelling in the backcountry, I have had several encounters and near encounters with both black and grizzly bears. Partially due to luck and partially due to the suggestions I offer here, none of these encounters have left me with more than a racing heart and a shaking hand.

First of all, it is extremely important that you are able to distinguish between blacks and grizzlies. Each has distinctly different behavioural patterns, and this affects the tactics you will use to avoid them. Do not rely on colour. Both species have several different, overlapping colour variations.

Generally, black bears are smaller, with a longer Roman-shaped (straight) nose and shorter front claws. They do not have a visible hump at the shoulder. Grizzlies tend to be much larger, and have a dish-shaped (concave) face, longer front claws, and a very distinct hump at the shoulder. If in doubt as to the species, assume it is the more dangerous grizzly.

Although both species are usually very timid and will run off at the sight or scent of humans, there is no guarantee that this will be every bear's reaction.

In Nahanni I have had both species pay me more than a passing interest. At Rabbitkettle a sub-adult grizzly took a shine to the warden station and on a couple of occasions came towards me after I had attempted to scare it off. On another occasion, at Scow Creek, a black bear exhibited such predatory behaviour we had to pelt it with rocks to stop it from approaching any closer. As it was, the bear continued to follow us, although from farther away. So there are no guarantees, just precautions to hedge your bet.

Your intelligence and ability to maintain self control while under pressure are your best defence. Notice that the use of firearms is not presented as an option for dealing with bears. Personally, I don't carry a firearm. I believe it is dangerous to rely on a gun to get you out of a jam. You have to be a good shot under extreme pressure, and guns are a hassle to carry and care for. Generally, I find them unnecessary. If you follow recommendations, you won't likely need a firearm except in the event of a surprise encounter, in which case you probably won't have time to use it anyway.

One of the most dangerous situations is to encounter a bear habituated to human food and to human presence. These bears are very dangerous because they have lost their fear of man and will approach quite close. If food is not available, they can become hostile and the chances of inadvertently finding yourself too close are much greater. Luckily, human impact in Nahanni has been limited, so it is unlikely that the bears in this area are habituated. This is not a guarantee, however; bears learn fast and a few mistakes with food and garbage can leave behind a potentially dangerous bear for the next party to happen upon.

The second most dangerous situation is to encounter a sow with cubs, and the third is to chance upon a bear protecting a food source.

Generally, grizzlies are more likely to be found above Virginia Falls, especially in the Rabbitkettle, Hole-in-the-Wall, Flat River confluence, and Glacier Lake areas. However, like black bears, they can be found throughout Nahanni. Black bears are especially prevalent on the Prairie Creek fan. Talk with the Rabbitkettle warden before you leave for the river and ask if there are any areas to be particularly concerned about.

Hiking in Bear Country Hike with your head up and be constantly aware of your surroundings. Like people, bears and other wildlife like to travel routes offering the least resistance. Are there fresh tracks or scats on the trail? Is there sign of a carcass nearby? Are there fresh dirt mounds from diggings? If so, look under the disturbed soil to see how withered the vegetation is; this will indicate the age of the diggings. Note any rocks that have recently been turned over or rotten logs that have been ripped open. Both of these indicate feeding by either blacks or grizzlies. Which way is the wind carrying your scent? Will it help to warn a bear if it is ahead of you? Or is the wind and nearby stream making too much noise to allow you to be heard?

Don't carry strong-smelling foods. Make lots of noise when you hike, especially in noisy areas such as banks of rushing streams and areas of dense bush which tend to muffle your presence. Be especially careful when you have a limited view of the route ahead. One fall, while hiking alone in a remote area of Kluane National Park, I came around a sharp bend in a heavy snow storm and stepped on three sets of *very* fresh grizzly tracks. In fact, at the side of the trail the branches were still swaying where the animals had left the path. The only thing that prevented me from a head-on with a sow grizzly and two cubs was my terrible singing! That was enough to convince me of the merits of this particular tactic. I don't suggest the use of bear bells or the like since for most of the time they will just drive you crazy or not ring loudly enough, thereby giving you a false sense of security. As an example: on one occasion I was on horseback after posting and closing a trail in Waterton Lakes National Park (because of an incident involving a grizzly), and was able to walk to within 20 feet of two approaching hikers before the horse and I startled them. They said they were relying on the bells to ward off danger. Wrong! Young adult bears can be quite curious of unusual sounds; bells, therefore, may actually attract them.

Be aware of the seasonal habits of bears. Steven Herrero's book, *Bear Attacks* offers some insight on this topic. The book will familiarize you with the bear's home turf and allow you to either avoid or to travel extra carefully in these areas.

If you see a bear from a long distance, and it hasn't yet seen you, quietly turn and detour out of there. If the bear has seen you, then your reaction will pretty much be determined by the bear's reaction. If the bear is aware of you but remains relatively unconcerned, quietly leave the area while waving your arms to help the bear identify what you are. **Never run**. The person who suggested running downhill from a bear obviously never had one pursue him in this manner; they run quite well downhill. The detection of bears through scent is also a myth. I have handled bears that were not at all strong smelling. Attempting to out-swim a bear is also not such a great idea as both blacks and grizzlies are excellent swimmers (see photo on page 171).

If a bear is relatively close and aware of you but showing no signs of aggression, then slowly back away and talk in slow calming tones. Don't stare at the bear since many predators consider this a challenge. Look for a good solid tree to climb should you need to. Of course, this won't do you any good if it's a black bear since they are excellent climbers. A word about trees. A good tree should be sufficiently solid to withstand a large bear trying to push it over, and it should have enough **small** branches for easy climbing. Grizzlies can also climb trees to a more limited extent by using larger branches. Climb high. One large adult grizzly has been known to climb as high as 16 feet using heavy branches for support. And even if they don't climb, grizzlies have a long reach.

If approached or charged by a grizzly here are a few of your options:

- As you slowly back away, drop an object such as a hat. Hopefully, the bear will stop to investigate the object, thus buying you some time.
- If a good climbing tree is nearby and the bear is 200 metres or more away you may still have time to climb to safety. A grizzly is capable of running 14 metres in a second!
- Another option is to stand your ground and face the bear, not letting it intimidate you, then slowly back away while yelling, making a loud noise, or deploying a bear repellent like cayenne spray or a bear banger.
- Move away and speak quietly while remaining non-threatening.
- Drop to the ground and play dead. Cover your head and neck with your hands and leave your pack on to provide some protection.
- Don't play dead unless you are definitely being attacked by a grizzly which perceives you as a threat. Being overtly aggressive is a valid response if the bear is a young adult and overly curious, or is old, sick or injured, or has been stalking you as prey. If the problem is caused by a black bear try the same tactics but act more aggressively if you think the bear perceives you as a threat.

Camping in Bear Country When selecting a campsite, take some time to scout around for signs of bears using the area. Here's a story to illustrate my point:

The second day out on a 900-kilometre canoe trip in the Yukon, my wife and I were looking to make camp. Knowing that the river had a salmon run on, I took my time to scout out a potential site. All was well, so we pitched camp. The next afternoon we laid low. Judy was in the tent having a siesta while I was slightly upriver, trying to catch a fish. I looked back at the campsite only to spot an adult grizzly opposite the camp on the other side of the river which was only about 10 metres wide at that point. I raced back to the tent, woke Judy, and asked her to pass me out the "bear banger" (a pencil-flare gun with a flare that explodes at the end of its flight; also known as a cracker shell). There was a mad flurry as she passed me the banger. By this time the bear had its front legs in the water and was heading directly for us. I took aim and BOOM, the shot exploded directly over the bear's head. Judging by the speed of the bear's departure, it should be somewhere near Anchorage by now! Curious of what attracted the bear, I scouted around again only to find that a salmon had washed up sometime during the previous night. I learned a valuable lesson, to say the least. Once an area seems clean never assume it will remain that way while you are there.

Having established camp, taking care not to set up on a game trail, the most important thing is to keep the campsite clean. This will not only help keep you safe, it will also protect those who follow after you. Once a bear has become habituated to human food it is very hard to stop it from coming back. Often the only recourse for wildlife managers is to destroy the bear. This happened to me just this spring when I was forced to destroy a sow black bear. Luckily, we were able to catch her pair of two-year-old cubs and relocate them but it nearly broke my heart when I released them from the trap. They fled a short distance, then sat, looked back and bawled for their mom. The whole mess was caused by campers who had left a can of peaches open on their picnic table while they went for a hike. The two cubs had introduced the sow to the treat and the hunt for human food was on.

When preparing your menu, try not to include odorous foods like bacon. Prepare all your meals far downwind of your tent, at least 75 metres away, and cache your food by suspending it from a rope slung between two trees, well off the ground, and far from the tent. Store items in plastic bags kept inside a nylon bag for added durability. This will help prevent the wind from dispersing the odours. In many of the park's designated campgrounds a food cache is provided. If no trees are present and there are no other caches, then leave the food etc. in airtight containers such as the barrels many paddlers use. Clean all dishes thoroughly. Any food bits left in the dishwater should be separated from the water, then either disposed of in the river or burned in a fire. Burn all your garbage to get rid of odours, remembering to pack out the remnants. I try to get rid of dishwater and smaller bits of food by slowly pouring them around a fire and allowing them to burn off. Cache garbage until you leave, don't bury it. If you spill food on your clothes or suspect that food odours have permeated them, cache your clothes as well. As a matter of course, I never take the clothes I cook in into my tent. Cache all toiletries including soap and toothpaste; don't take them into your tent. I know of one occasion when a black bear ripped into a tent and ate hemorrhoid cream! Some people even have separate tents for winter and summer since odours from winter cooking in their tents have permeated the fabric.

Women travelling in the backcountry during their menstrual cycle should be aware of potential problems. Use tampons and be very careful with disposal. Either burn them very thoroughly or pack them out wrapped in two or three plastic bags that seal very well.

Personally, even with the knowledge that I have done everything possible to prevent an attack, I still plan possible escape strategies. Into my tent I take my "bear banger" with extra shells, a knife in case I have to cut a new door, and a flashlight. Before retiring for the evening I have a look for any trees nearby that may provide refuge. I also leave my canoe ready for a quick getaway. Around the seats I fasten the whitewater fanny packs mentioned earlier, the lifejackets, a day pack with additional clothes, and the paddles. Theoretically, all we would have to do is turn over the canoe, get it into the water, and push off.

Recommended Book:

Herrero, S. **Bear Attacks: Their Causes and Avoidance** Winchester Press, Piscataway, NJ. 1985.

Hypothermia

Hypothermia, a progressive lowering of the body's core temperature, is responsible for the majority of wilderness fatalities. Therefore it is important to recognize the signs and symptoms at an early stage and treat the patient correctly. There are two stages. The first involves all or some of the following symptoms:

- uncontrollable shivering
- pale, cool skin
- loss of ability to perform simple tasks such as doing up a zipper
- frequent stumbling, clumsy paddling
- patients may deny that they are in trouble

If diagnosed at this early stage, hypothermia can be effectively treated, though the process may take several hours depending on the severity of the condition. Treatment at this stage includes:

- remove the patient from the source of cold. Get out of the wind, rain and water as soon as possible.
- give warm, sweet drinks, though very little heating of the body core can be achieved this way.
- allow the person to vigorously rewarm himself/herself if he/she is able to do so by activity.
- remove all wet clothing and place the person in a warm sleeping bag with another stripped person if the severity warrants it. Skin-to-skin contact is very effective. Concentrate on warming the trunk while allowing the extremities to warm more slowly. You might also consider putting the person in a tent in which the air has been warmed with heated rocks.
- have the person exhale into a piece of cloth, such as a toque, and then inhale the already warmed air.
- DO NOT administer alcohol; this will only worsen the condition.
- monitor the person's recovery; the 24 hour period following treatment is critical since relapse is possible. Another reduction in body temperature could be very serious.

In advanced hypothermia the person appears exhausted and is unable to rise after a rest. His/her speech is slow, slurred and incoherent. As the condition deepens, shivering stops, indicating the body's inability to combat the cold (not to be confused with the cessation of shivering of a recovering victim; that person will be much more alert). If the victim has reached this stage the situation is serious. There is very little that can be done to reverse hypothermia in the field at this point. However, here are some points to consider:

- treat the patient very gently; any rough treatment during evacuation could cause the heart to stop beating effectively (fibrillate).
- prevent any further heat loss with a sleeping bag, warmed tent etc.
- Whether you carry out an improvised evacuation depends on the size and ability of the party, location, weather etc. Seek assistance from the wardens or outfitters who have radios as soon as possible to arrange for evacuation to medical care.

Contending with Emergencies

Any number of emergencies can befall you. This section directs you towards an appropriate course of action, or at least gets you thinking in that direction. At the very minimum, you should consider having at least two persons in your party with current training in at least basic first aid and Cardio-Pulmonary Resuscitation (CPR). More comprehensive medical training, such as a wilderness medical technician certificate or equivalent, is very desirable.

In the Air

There isn't much chance you will run into an emergency in the air. But you never know for sure — the weather in the mountains can get plenty ugly, plenty fast. Before you take off, ask the pilot to show you where the Emergency Locator Transmitter (ELT) is kept on the plane. In addition, get him or her to show you where the other emergency equipment is stored. By law they are required to carry a first-aid kit, signal flares, and emergency camping equipment. Float planes also require flotation devices for all occupants. After going over the safety equipment, get a run-down on the emergency procedures suggested by the pilot. Don't worry about feeling stupid for forecasting doom; these actions may save your life and the lives of others.

If you do crash, consider the following:

- Secure your own safety first; you won't be of any use if you become a casualty.
- Secure the safety of others. Depending on conditions, i.e. threat of fire, you may have to get people away from the plane. Administer first aid.
- Make sure the ELT is operating. It turns on automatically on impact. Beware of turning it off by mistake.
- Stabilize the situation. Pilots file a flight plan so that rescue efforts will be initiated if they are overdue. Depending on weather conditions, a response should come quite quickly, usually within a day. Your priorities are to prevent worsening of victims injuries, and to prevent dehydration and hypothermia. Make use of food, sleeping bags, and tents.
- Prepare to signal. Use flares, a signal mirror, smoke from a fire (three fires is internationally recognized as a distress) or anything you can improvise.

In the Water

Before you start your river trip, you and your party should practice some basic river-rescue techniques and develop a group strategy in case a canoe flips over.

Here are a few suggestions:

- Don't let go of your paddle unless you are sure it can be retrieved, or if holding it will prevent you from being rescued. If possible, stow it in your boat.

- Hold onto the upstream part of the canoe to keep it from being pushed over you or pinning you against a rock or other obstacle. If you are in a rocky rapid, such as below Moose Ponds, let the canoe ride lengthwise through the rocks. This will help prevent broaching.

- Swim the canoe to shore if there are no other boats available to assist. In these frigid temperatures you will only have a few minutes before hypothermia causes you to lose control of your limbs. If necessary, abandon your canoe and get ashore before this happens. Let another canoe rescue your boat. Luckily, on the South Nahanni there are usually bends in the river to bring you closer to shore. Forget trying to perform a canoe-over-canoe rescue since there will be too much gear tied into the boat.

- In the event you find yourself floating through a set of rapids, remember to float on your back with your feet pointing downstream and on the surface where they won't get hung-up on underwater obstructions. In this position you will be more able to protect yourself from collisions with rocks etc. Try to swim into quiet water or an eddy by heading straight for shore and never try to stand up in fast-moving water until it is too shallow to swim in. Use a throw bag to retrieve someone from the water.

- If you expect to spend some time in the water before rescue, try to conserve body heat. Do up all your clothing and curl into a fetal position. If in a group, huddle together. Do not try to exercise in an effort to keep warm as this will only dissipate heat faster.

- Get warm and dry clothes on as soon as possible. If none are available, wring as much water as you can from your wet clothes and get a fire going. Assign a dry member of the party to watch for symptoms of hypothermia. Wearing a wet suit and wet boots will help protect you from hypothermia.

On Land

The same principles hold true. Ensure your own safety first, then treat the injured hiker to the best of your ability, including treatment for shock. Watch for hypothermia, even on hot summer days. Transport the patient to medical help or, if the situation is more serious, send a member of your party to bring help to you. Remain with the patient at all times unless the situation offers you no alternative but to go for help yourself.

Emergency Communications for Additional Assistance

In some instances you may require help from outside your own party. In the national park, the park wardens are the primary agency for search-and-rescue. Outside the park, contact the RCMP. Remember, help could be a week or more away depending on location and season. It may be better in some instances to solicit help from fellow paddlers or from outfitter guides who are excellent candidates, having medical training and access to emergency radios.

If you need additional assistance:

- request assistance through other paddlers (also known as the "Moccasin Telegraph"). This is the most common method used. If you cannot remain on the river bank to signal help, use flagging tape or other material to attract attention. If an accident happens upstream of the park, get the park warden stationed at Rabbitkettle Lake to radio for assistance. If an accident happens downstream of Rabbitkettle, contact the nearest occupied warden station at Nahanni Butte (radio and telephone).
- signal over-flying aircraft using flares, smoke etc.
- use an emergency locator device.

When you dispatch someone for help make sure to send the following information out with them:

- your location, using precise information such as a map-grid reference or well-known location name such as "at the confluence of the South Nahanni and Broken Skull Rivers".
- the nature of the emergency, e.g. stranded without gear. This should include a description of any medical conditions that may exist, the date and time the accident occurred, and the number of people injured or ill. If you are not sure what the medical problem is, indicate the mechanism or circumstances surrounding the injury or illness. This will allow rescuers to better prepare for dealing with the emergency.
- the number of members in your party and, if some have been dispatched to get help, their location/destination.
- the kind of equipment you have on hand, i.e. stove, first-aid equipment, tent, sleeping bags, food. Include the colour of some of the larger pieces of equipment more likely to be spotted from the air, such as "a red tent and a green canoe."

Recommended Books:

McKown, Doug **Canoeing Safety and Rescue** Rocky Mountain Books, Calgary 1992.

Mason, Bill **Path of the Paddle: An illustrated Guide to the Art of Paddling** Key Porter Books 1984

Steele, Peter **Far from Help** Cloudcap, Seattle 1991.

Wilkerson, James A., Bangs, Cameron, Hayward, John A. **Hypothermia, Frostbite and other Cold Injuries** The Mountaineers, Seattle 1986.

Forgey, William W. **Hypothermia, Death by Exposure** ACS Books, Merrillville 1985.

Setnicka, Tim J. **Wilderness Search and Rescue** Appalachian Mountain Club, Boston 1980.

Emergency phone numbers	
Park wardens, Fort Simpson	695-3151
RCMP at Fort Simpson	695-3111
RCMP at Fort Liard	770-4221

Overleaf: First Canyon.

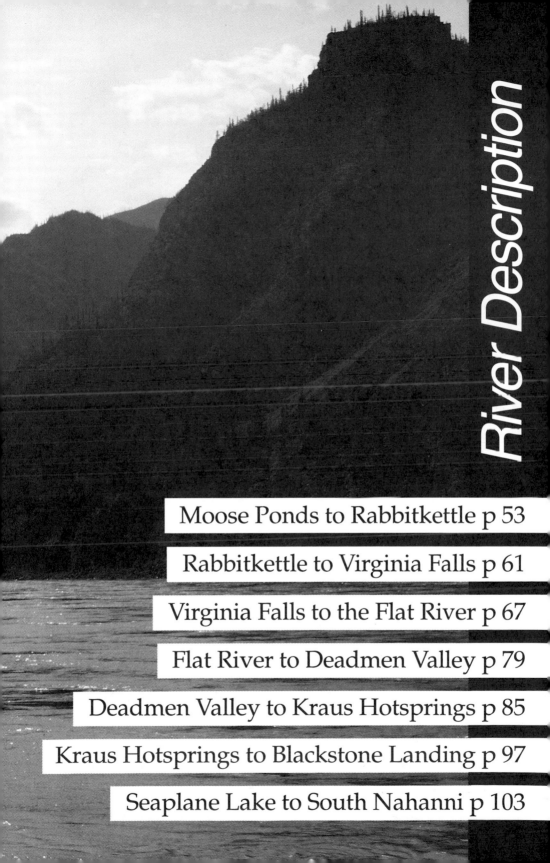

River Description

An aerial view of the Moose Ponds.

The upper South Nahanni showing Dave and Debbie's sled which was used to access Moose Ponds. Solitary Mount Wilson looms on the horizon.

Moose Ponds to Rabbitkettle

**maps
1-8**

Approximate distances

Moose Ponds to end of whitewater, 60 km
end of whitewater to Island Lake, 58 km
Island Lake to Broken Skull River, 47 km
Broken Skull River to Rabbitkettle Lake trail, 48 km

Total approximate distance, 213 km

This is the most challenging section of the South Nahanni. Rapids are likely class IV in the spring, lessening in severity throughout the summer until they become too shallow to run by mid-August, depending on the year. Departing from ponds near treeline, the river enters a post-glacial valley cut through the Logan Mountains, passing such landmarks as the Little Nahanni River, Moore's Cabin and Hotspring [80], Broken Skull River, and Brintnell Creek which accesses the world famous Cirque of the Unclimbables [3]. On your right the views of the Ragged Range are spectacular. Although this section can be paddled in about 5 days, one week allows a more leisurely pace with time for side hikes, stops at points of interest, bad weather, accidental swims etc.

In order to describe this section I will recount the notes and observations made by Hal Morrison and myself during July 3 to 7, 1987. The purpose of our trip was to properly map the location of the rapids in this 213-kilometre section since previous descriptions were erroneous and were causing some paddlers grief. The rapid rating assigned to each rapid was our interpretation based on the water levels we encountered at that time and the rating system described previously. Although I often refer to rock avoidance, ledges and tricky hydraulics were present in some of the rapids as well. It's best to scout the rapid for yourself anyway!

July 3

Arrived at Moose Ponds at 4:15 pm. Nice campsite, well used, on the larger lake. Two adult trumpeter swans on the second lake. Paddled through a series of ponds. Entered a small outlet and paddled a short distance to the main stream. Encountered sections of easy class I riffles extending to camp one at the first major creek entering on river left. Nice spot! Time taken — 2.25 hours from the start.

Initiation Rapid (class III) lives up to its name, introducing paddlers to a long stretch of tricky whitewater.

July 4

Left camp one at 9 am. At 9:25 saw Deb and Dave's sled standing on river left. At 11:00 encountered a major creek on river left. Up to here, we paddled through easy class I with lots of rocks.

At 11:15 stopped and put on spray skirt, then ran class II with lots of rocks. At 11:20 encountered Initiation Rapid, class III with lots of rock avoidance. Continuous class II. At 11:25 encountered Descente Rapid, class II-III. Small cliff with cliff swallow nests at river right just below the rapid. Ran easy class II-III till 1:30 pm. Somewhere in here was Thread the Needle Rapid which was indistinguishable from the rest of the rapids. Creek entered on river right. Large cliff with cliff-swallow nests on river right. Continued paddling class II-III. Somewhere in here was Danish Dynamite Rapid, which (again) was indistinguishable from the rest of the rapids.

At 3:15 we encountered a large stream entering on river left and Junction Rapid. Tricky class III+ with lots of rock avoidance. At approximately 4 pm a large creek entered on river right. Two sets of class III+, called Bailing Rapids, occurred right after the creek.

Set up camp two at the next stream entering on river right at approximately 5 pm. What a riot! Excellent paddling! No swims and only one serious rock kiss! Oooh La La – gotta do this again! (We were punch-drunk from having concentrated on quickly approaching rocks for so long. Back-paddling was not in our repertoire of paddling skills!)

Moore's Hotspring and Cabin [80]

Moore's Hotspring, accessed by a side channel of the river, provides cold, tired paddlers with a warm spot to soak away their pains. The temperature is undoubtedly in the thirties (Celsius) and near the spring source the water is hot enough to burn your skin. This is the warmest of the hotsprings you'll encounter on your trip, *except* during flood conditions when the Nahanni backs up into the spring and makes it too cold for a pleasurable soak. The soils in the area benefit from the heated earth which in turn supports a very lush growth of cow parsnip and other species. By the way, mosquitos love it here too!

right:
Exploring the lush vegetation around Moore's Hotspring.

bottom: Moore's cabin lies abandoned about one kilometre upstream of the hotspring. John and Joanne Moore built this honeymoon cabin in 1978 to escape the hustle and bustle of the modern world for one year.

Hollywood Rapid.

July 5

Left camp two at 9:00 am, carried by easy class I. At 9:45 encountered Hollywood Rapid and The Sequel. Most serious rapids encountered so far — class III++. Fast, lots of rocks, serious ledges with hydraulics. The second one was worse than the first and located 200 metres below. Scout this one! Paddled class II+ with large standing waves and large troughs. At 11:15 a large stream entered from river left — end of continuous white water. Calm water from here. Paddled for three hours in the rain. Made camp near stream entering on river right.

July 6

More rain! Paddled three hours to Moore's Hotspring. One area is extremely hot — cooler where the river mixes in. Moore's cabin was quite dirty with pack rat turds. I wouldn't be too keen to sleep in here! It's a six hour paddle to our next camp at Broken Skull River. Elbow Rapid at the 90° bend to the southeast woke me up but it was nothing to worry about.

July 7

Beautiful sunny day. A half day paddle to the sign indicating Nahanni National Park. Couple of hours back passed Brintnell Creek — wish we had time for the hike to Glacier Lake. You have to stay to river right after passing the sign otherwise you run the risk of taking the wrong channel and missing the trail to Rabbitkettle Lake campground 4 km downstream. It's an easy portage of about 600 metres. Some people are camping on the downstream tip of the island opposite the trail, a good spot if water levels aren't too high. (Note: sign in at the check-in station located at the river end of the trail and if you haven't already done so, register your trip with the warden at the warden cabin.)

Hike 1 Mount Wilson (map 1)

Mount Wilson (2275 m) marks the origin of the South Nahanni River where it exits Moose Ponds. Consequently the mountain offers excellent views of this part of the river and of the surrounding valleys. Your target is the southeast ridge. Use the trail that begins on the west side of the second pond to get to the foot of the mountain, then scramble up the scree slopes to gain the ridge. A fairly low-angle slope of broken rock leads to the top. This is a fairly tough hike of about 7 kilometres with round trips taking as much as 10.5 hours. Bring your own water.

Right: A view of Mount Wilson from Moose Ponds. The hike ascends the left skyline. Experienced hikers can also scramble up the slightly steeper northwest ridge (right skyline) to make a loop.

Bottom: The summit ridge.

Photo: Keith Morton

Photo: Doug Eastcott

Hike 2 Glacier Lake, Cirque of the Unclimbables (map 7)

This hike from the river to the beautiful blue-green waters of Glacier Lake is roughly a 18 kilometre, 5 to 6 hour round trip of moderately strenuous trekking.

From the mouth of Brintnell Creek follow the bank of the South Nahanni upstream using an indistinct trail with plenty of blazes. Hike for about one kilometre until you reach a snye (or back channel) in the river. Look for a heavily blazed pine tree. From here, the trail turns and heads southwest. Follow it over the hills to Brintnell Creek, then west along the north bank of the creek to the main lake. The boreal forest is quite a bush-thrash in places and it is easy to lose the trail or confuse it with game trails.

At Glacier Lake, Nahanni River Adventures and Black Feather Outfitters have cached an old canoe for use in paddling across the lake, a welcome alternative to fighting through the bush to the other end. You will have to bring your own lifejackets and paddles. As a matter of courtesy please consult these outfitter before using the canoe: their addresses and phone numbers are included in the "Planning Your Trip" chapter on page 15. If a canoe is available, count on spending at least three days getting to the cirque and back from the South Nahanni.

There is a well-worn campsite at the far end of the lake where two streams enter from the west. By following the most northerly of the streams, a hiker plods up steep terrain for two or three hours into the alpine flowers of Fairy Meadow. From the cirque you are treated to magnificent views of the Unclimbables, a cathedral of towering granite walls jutting straight up from the valley floor for hundreds of metres and a challenge to mountaineers from around the world. There are two things to be careful of here: grizzlies and falling rock.

Besides foraging grizzlies, the towering walls and talus slopes are home to a variety of alpine wildlife, including whistling pikas and Golden eagles. Mount Sir James MacBrien, at 2764 m in height, is the highest of the peaks, most of which are visible from Rabbitkettle Lake as you will see. This area and Nahanni Needles, located near Hole-in-the-Wall Lake, offer the best rock climbing opportunities in the park; the rest of the region has very crumbly sedimentary rock. Rock climbing is not the only challenge available. Hiking in this rough country can tax even the strongest of backpackers.

For an account of the natural processes that led to the formation of Cirque of the Unclimbables [3] see on pages 139 and 140.

Opposite: Bustle Tower in Cirque of the Unclimbables. It was first climbed in 1973 by Joe Bridges, Sandy Bill and Galen Rowell via the lefthand skyline ridge.

Rabbitkettle to Virginia Falls

**maps
9-14**

Approximate distances

Park boundary to Rabbitkettle River 4 km
*Rabbitkettle River to Hell Roaring Creek (use attached map,
the topographic map has this creek mislabelled) 37 km*
Hell Roaring Creek to Flood Creek 15 km
Flood Creek to high prominent cut bank on river right 33 km
Cut bank to Sunblood warden cabin 18 km
Sunblood warden cabin to Virginia Falls campground 10 km

Total approximate distance 117 km

The paddle from Rabbitkettle to Virginia Falls is quite slow, taking a full two days. At the Rabbitkettle end are some sections of faster water with boils — nothing to worry about though. Throughout this section the river slowly winds its way through a wide post glacial valley in the Mackenzie Mountains, quite different in character to the canyons of the lower sections. You are quite close to the alpine here and there are a number of interesting hikes leaving river left. I have found this section particularly good for viewing wildlife such as bear, moose and the occasional lynx, especially in the early morning and at dusk.

Along the way Hell Roaring Creek and Flood Creek [50] are popular camping destinations. It becomes increasingly difficult to find good campsites the nearer you get to Virginia Falls. Ten kilometres before the falls you pass Sunblood warden cabin. Have your camera ready. Just below the cabin on river left Dall's sheep can often be seen at a mineral lick [60].

Depending on the wind, you may hear the roar of Virginia Falls as you approach the campground location about 500 metres above the Sluice Box. Look for a sign and the check-in kiosk on river right. The river is very slow at this point so there should be no worry about being swept into the falls. Several campsites are within an easy walk of the landing. In recent years the whole camping area has been extensively rebuilt to reduce impact on the area. Note: camping is not permitted at the falls themselves.

*Opposite top: Skinny dipping in Rabbitkettle Lake: in the background are
the peaks of the Ragged Range. photo: Doug Eastcott*

Opposite bottom: Relaxing on the upper river near Sunblood warden cabin.

Hike 3 Rabbitkettle Hotsprings (map 9)

Located near the western boundary of the park, Rabbitkettle Hotsprings has formed at the junction of the Nahanni and Rabbitkettle Valleys. Two tufa mounds, differing in form, were created by two springs and together comprise the largest formations of their kind in Canada and possibly the largest in the world at this northerly latitude.

To see the hotsprings, visitors must accompany the Rabbitkettle warden who conducts informal guided tours. These tours are usually run twice a day, so if your time is limited be sure to check the schedule beforehand at the Fort Simpson office. Don't pass up the opportunity to go on this hike!

The 5 kilometre trail rambles over easy terrain and usually takes between three and four hours return. Along the way, visitors get excellent views of piping sinkholes [59], both dry and filled with water the colour of jade, many different kinds of wildlife, and a wide variety of plants associated with aspen/conifer forest.

Once you're at the springs the warden escorts small groups of visitors barefoot along a specific path to the top of North Mound and, in shoes, to South Mound. These careful measures are necessary to ensure the mounds aren't damaged. Currently, a study is assessing the damage caused by visitors and it's possible that walks on the mounds may be discontinued in the future.

Both mounds are built of tufa, a soft sandstone-like material consisting of mainly calcium carbonate which has been deposited from spring waters. The North Mound is by far the most dramatic of the two with its 70 metre diameter and 20 metre high walls. It is free standing unlike the less spectacular but no less interesting South Mound which has developed into a hillside. While on the mound look for natural objects such as feathers and leaves that are slowly being entombed in the tufa. Imagine the story the mounds could tell if you were able to see them in cross-section — 10,000 years of natural history recorded in their walls.

A description of the process involved in the growth of the mounds [58] and the mechanics of piping sinkholes is presented on page 165.

Opposite top: Rabbitkettle Hotsprings. The summit of North Mound.

Opposite bottom: North Mound from the air showing gours and rimstone dams.

Hikes 4a & b Secret Lakes (map 11)

Secret Lakes consists of a group of small but deep, jade-coloured lakes tucked into a steep-sided mountain valley. There are two possible routes. The first one, Hike 4a, departs from a high bank on the South Nahanni immediately below and opposite the point where the Rabbitkettle River enters the South Nahanni and involves hiking through muskeg and along creek beds and game trails to gain a low pass leading straight to the lakes. This is a 12 kilometre return trip which takes about 9 hours.

The second route (Hike 4b) follows the creek bed that meets the Nahanni roughly 14 kilometres below the Rabbitkettle portage. This route is somewhat longer, 20 kilometres return, but is less strenuous and so takes the same amount of time.

An aerial view of Secret Lakes. Hike 4a goes through the narrow gap at bottom left. The ridge above the lakes is traversed by Hike 5.

Hike 5 Alpine Ridge Hike (map 11)

This is an enjoyable and strenuous hike along a horseshoe-shaped ridge separating Secret Lakes from the creek located to the east which is mislabelled on older topographic maps (1:250,000) as Hell Roaring Creek. The ridge reaches a maximum height of approximately 2150 metres and offers spectacular views of Rabbitkettle Lake, the Rabbitkettle valley, and the South Nahanni Valley. Irvine Valley appears to the southeast where small glacier-carved lakes are evident [61]. From here to Sunblood, the valley gets wider and access to the alpine becomes much more difficult, so take advantage of this opportunity to enjoy the views.

The start of the hike is located on the left side of the river opposite an island. Look carefully and you should be able to distinguish an alluvial fan through the trees. Once on the fan, head up the stream bed until the drainage becomes constricted, then continue up the ridge on the left. Hike along scree ridges to the highest point then follow the horseshoe-shaped ridge, trending east, then southeast, which returns you to the head of the same stream you started up. The entire hike of about 27 kilometres should take 6 to 8 hours return, with shorter versions possible. Remember to take water with you.

View back along the summit ridge.

65

photo: Doug Eastcott

An aerial view of Virginia Falls, showing portage trail.

Virginia Falls above Fourth Canyon.

Virginia Falls
to the Flat River

**maps
15-16**

Approximate distances

Virginia Falls campground to Marengo Creek campground, 8 km
Marengo Creek campground to Clearwater Creek, 6 km
Clearwater Creek to Figure 8, 7 km
Figure 8 to Wrigley Creek, 1 km
Wrigley Creek to Flat River confluence, 9 km

Total approximate distance, 30 km

This 30 km stretch is quite thrilling with rapids in Fourth Canyon and at Figure 8 to challenge your paddling skills and a fast current throughout. Try to slow down and enjoy the canyon scenery. Barring any mishaps this section takes one full day. Add extra time if portaging Figure 8 Rapid.

Don't start your portage around Virginia Falls from the campground. Believe it or not, I've seen people do this! Spare yourself some grief. Although the start of the portage may look too close to the Sluice Box, there is lots of room to pull out safely, and the 1.2 kilometre trek from this point into Fourth Canyon is far enough! Paddle the right side of the river from the campground to where the portage sign stands about 30 m above the Sluice Box. Be careful; this is not the place to practise swimming. Expect loose boards on the board-walks and slippery conditions. When you leave gear unattended during the portage make sure everything is zipped up and secure from the local ravens who know all the tricks for getting at food and often leave quite a mess.

Fourth Canyon Rapids

For five kilometres Fourth Canyon offers almost continuous white water ranging from class I-III. There are very few rocks to avoid although I once saw an inflatable kayak virtually explode its occupants and gear into the river after hitting the first rock possible! The difficulty lies in the river's speed, the huge standing waves, and the occasional bad hydraulics, especially at high water near the canyon walls which protrude into the river. In most cases the largest of the standing waves can be avoided, but a spray skirt is still essential, except during low water levels. There are several opportunities for getting to shore should you need to do some bailing, take a pee break, or whatever.

Taking off from the portage trail below the falls, be careful the current doesn't push you into the canyon wall and large standing waves at the outside bend immediately below the trail. To avoid this, walk your loaded canoe upriver past the portage. This will give you some additional paddling time. Then jump in and paddle like hell in a front ferry to the other side of the river (or as far as you like), point the bow downriver and enjoy the ride!

At low water levels the rapids are not nearly so spectacular, but at least you'll have time to enjoy the scenery. At very low water levels there are a couple of ledges near the end of the canyon you should keep an eye out for.

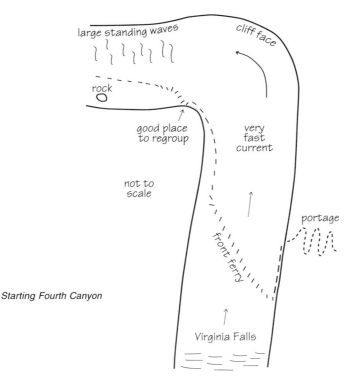

Marengo Creek campground is located on river left below the canyon opposite Marengo Creek.

Clearwater Creek

At high water levels there are absolutely huge standing waves — the largest on the entire river — located opposite the creek mouth. If you have the time to play, empty the canoe and take a run at these skyrockets, but be prepared to swim. To avoid them stay to river left and you should have no problem.

Opposite top: Getting organized at the trail end of the Virginia Falls portage.
Opposite bottom: Fourth Canyon showing rapids.

Figure 8 Rapid

Also known as Hell's Gate, this can be the trickiest rapid in the park. Don't worry; if you don't like the look of it, especially if you are a single-canoe party, you can take the portage as shown on the next diagram.

The river bends sharply to the right as you approach the rapid, then makes a 90° turn to the left. The water moves quite quickly, lots of it smashing into the canyon wall and peeling off to the left. The rest turns right into a large eddy. The hazards in this rapid are large standing waves, unstable hydraulics and boils, and the threat of being pushed into the canyon wall. This is no rapid to play around on. Take the time to scout it.

To get to the portage trail stay river right as you approach the rapid. The current will take you into the large eddy and the trail. Be watchful for logs and other debris circulating in the eddy. The portage trail offers a good vantage point from which to scout the Figure 8.

Figure 8 Rapid

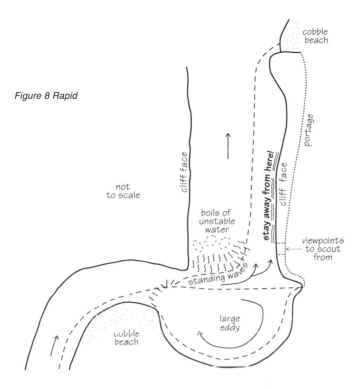

Figure 8 Rapid

To run the Figure 8 from the portage trail, use the eddy to take you around to the top of the rapid. From here, front ferry into the main current. Spin around and skirt the edge of the standing waves on the upstream side. Turn the canoe and paddle through the last couple of standing waves and into a current that will carry you downriver. Stay away from the wall at all costs.

In this rapid, I have seen strong hydraulics pull a buoyant canoe underwater for several minutes. Imagine what could happen to an even less buoyant person! That said, Figure 8 is really quite straightforward. I have paddled it at least a dozen times and have never been dumped, and by no means do I consider myself an expert paddler. However, the consequences of a swim here could be serious.

Like all rapids on the Nahanni, Figure 8 changes temperament with variations in the water level. At high water the rapid can be horrendous with huge standing waves and large whirlpools. At low water, it is much less severe. On one occasion when the normal route through the rapid looked much too serious we decided to take the sharp inside corner which appeared more appealing even though the current remained very strong. We front-ferried from the eddy over to the far wall and tucked into the inside corner. The force of the water felt as though it would pull our arms off but we made it through, thanks to a well-placed low brace by my wife, Judy.

Wrigley Creek Whirlpool

Immediately after passing Wrigley Creek there are two or three islands (depending on water levels) on the left side of the river. At river right in the main channel and at the far end of the island is a very nasty, canoe-sucking whirlpool, a rotating river-hole which has sent many paddlers into the drink. If water levels permit, stay to the left of the islands. If this route has dried up, take the channel between the islands but hug the left side since anywhere else will push the canoe towards the whirlpool.

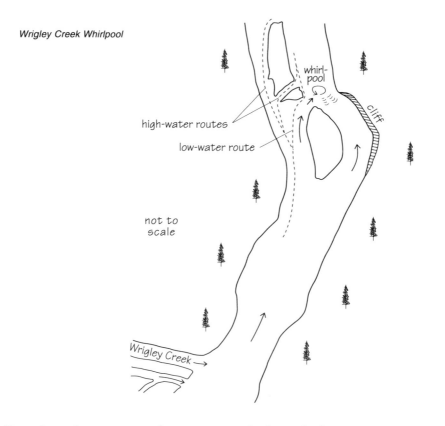

Wrigley Creek Whirlpool

From here the current pushes you towards the end of a very enjoyable day. There are several good places to camp, the most popular being at the confluence of the Flat and South Nahanni Rivers.

In case of emergency, the Flat River warden cabin is located on river left up the Flat River a short distance above the braids at the confluence. It is patrolled on a regular basis by the wardens.

Opposite: Marengo Falls.

Hike 6 Marengo Falls (map 15)

Using a compass and map, bushwhack to Marengo Creek from the Virginia Falls campground, then hike *downstream* to the falls. Be prepared to get wet feet from hummocky moss and muskeg. While hiking along the creek, keep an eye out for the pair of Ziess binoculars I lost in 1986. Finders keepers! This is also where I had the macho contest with the bull caribou I mention on page 170. The 30 metre falls are most impressive when seen from below. This 6 kilometre round trip should take between 3.5 and 4.5 hours, but take your time and explore the creek more thoroughly.

photo: Keith Morton

Virginia Falls from the brink, showing Mason Rock in the upper half of the photo.

Hike 7 Virginia Falls (map 15)

Virginia Falls is a gentle river gone mad. Cyclones of foaming water explode atop house-sized rocks in a confused 90 metre plunge into Fourth Canyon. This is one of the most amazing of Nahanni's many spectacular features. Trails and viewpoints offer several excellent opportunities to lose yourself in the rampage.

The central pillar of rock which pierces the falls has informally been named Mason Rock after Bill Mason, paddler, artist, filmmaker, and friend of the Nahanni.

There are a number of excellent spots from which to view the falls and Sluice Box Rapids [41]. The distance is only about 3 kilometres return from the campground, but with so much to see this could take most of the day! Be very careful on the slippery rocks and sometimes muddy trails. I've heard horror stories of people who have slipped into the water; luckily, always managing to pull themselves out. Depending on the weather, there can be a bounty of blueberries to sample and wildflowers to photograph in the falls area.

Named in 1929 after an early explorer's daughter, the falls were created through a complex history of erosion, burial, and rebirth spanning thousands of years. The chapter "A Unique Landscape" provides a more thorough description. See [40] on page 147.

Sluice Box Rapids from the trail. For another view see the photo on the title page.

Hike 8 Sunblood Mountain (map 15)

The hike to Sunblood Mountain (1615 m) starts directly opposite Virginia Falls campground. After paddling across the river and securing your canoe, pick one of the many informal trails leading to the scree slopes on the south shoulder of the mountain. Hike up the scree and then the southeast ridge to the summit. From the top, the differences between glaciated terrain (up-river view) and unglaciated terrain (down-river view) become very apparent. The round-trip distance is 16 kilometres which takes 5 to 6 hours. Take water with you.

While on the south bank of the Nahanni, hike to Virginia Falls for a completely different perspective.

Left: Sunblood Mountain from the portage trail. Trails lead above the cliffs to the base of the southeast ridge which is followed from right to left to the summit.

Bottom: View from the summit of Sunblood Mountain of the South Nahanni and Virginia Falls. Hike 7 and the portage trail are clearly visible. photo: Keith Morton.

Photo: D. Salayka

Upper Virginia Falls with Mason Rock at centre.
Photo taken from the north bank near the trail up Sunblood Mountain.

Flat River to Deadmen Valley

maps 17-19

Approximate distances

Flat River to Mary River, 14 km
Mary River to The Gate and Pulpit Rock, 15 km
The Gate and Pulpit Rock to Big Bend campground, 21 km
Big Bend campground to start of Second Canyon, 1 km
start of Second Canyon to Headless Creek, 17 km
Headless Creek to Deadmen Valley campground, 12 km

Total approximate distance, 80 km

This section is easily paddled in two days, the river remaining quite fast, requiring very little paddling. There are currents and boils that require you to remain slightly on guard, but for the most part you can relax and allow the river to show you her treasures. Take your time, pull out and explore. There are many more hiking possibilities than are described.

The entrance of the Flat River marks the start of Third Canyon where the river cuts through the Funeral Range. A little downstream of the junction at river left look for strange rounded bulges of rock protruding from shale cliffs just above the water level. Further along are other interesting geological formations such as The Gate, Pulpit Rock, and Big Bend. Twin Falls, located just downstream from The Gate, provides an invigorating natural shower. If camping at Big Bend, look for claw marks on the bear tree.

Second Canyon is even more impressive with its Great Spur. From here a number of hikes lead into the Headless Range. After passing the infamous Headless Valley be careful in the braided channels entering Deadmen Valley, and keep an eye out for log jams and sweepers. On river left you pass a series of rotational slumps with drunken forests. Prairie Creek fan and the Tlogot-sho Plateau mark the end of this section.

Opposite the upstream end of Prairie Creek fan you'll see the old forestry cabin. This is Deadmen Valley campsite and check-in station. Take a look at the miniature carved paddles in the cabin that bear the names of previous paddlers. About 20 or so metres downstream on the same side is the Deadmen Valley warden cabin. Some paddlers prefer to camp on Prairie Creek fan — there's lots of room.

Opposite top: An aerial view of Third Canyon and The Gate.
Opposite bottom: Passing through The Gate. Pulpit Rock on the left.

Hike 9 The Gate Viewpoint (map 18)

The short hike to the canyon rim overlooking the Gate offers an interesting and scary perspective of this rather unusual landform. From the top are excellent views of the canyon walls, Pulpit Rock [39], and the river. See if you can decipher the events that led the river to adopt this course. You should be able to distinguish the old river meander [38] mentioned in "A Unique Landscape" on page 147.

From the camping area, upstream of the Gate on river left, the trail follows the creek valley for a short distance, then climbs the backside of the hill to the canyon rim. Hike the rim to the top on a steep path that requires sure footing. Allow 2 to 3 hours for the round trip.

Opposite top: Downstream of The Gate, showing Pulpit Rock and the warden's patrol boat.

Opposite bottom: Scenery typical of Second and Third Canyons.

Right top: Pulpit Rock from the canyon rim. Note the canoe. Photo: Keith Morton

Bottom: View upstream of The Gate, showing hill climbed by Hike 9.

Hike 10 Big Bend to the Headless Range (map 18)

The hike up this unnamed valley from the mouth of the unnamed side creek offers a pleasant side trip. The hiking is easy to begin with, but good footwear is recommended since the route involves walking on rounded boulders. If the weather's hot and you feel like taking a dip in pools of cool water or slipping down some natural water slides, take the first tributary entering the stream from the right (looking upstream). This route is a little more difficult but you can turn around at any time you like.

For those of you who are truly ambitious and able to overcome the logistical problems, continue up the tributary stream and then climb the broad scree slope (steep and loose) leading to the spine of the Headless Range at about 1700 m. This is the most difficult part of the hike. By hiking south along the ridge you end up at Headless Creek where, hopefully, your comrades are waiting with your canoe. This is a fairly tough and dry hike of about 23 kilometres, so take plenty of water. The views, however, are fantastic and well worth the effort. To complete the entire hike, a very long day of sustained effort with a light pack is required. Another warden and I completed this route in reverse (i.e., Headless Creek to Big Bend) in a day and a half after having spent a night out on the ridge. For those hikers who wish to get high with a little less effort, I suggest you consider Hike 11.

View from Big Bend of the Headless Range. Extended route follows the skyline ridge from left to right.

Hike 11 Headless Range via Scow Creek (map 18)

This 16 kilometre, 7 hour round trip offers spectacular views of Deadmen Valley and Second Canyon from a 1390 m summit of the Headless Range. Though a fairly strenuous hike with lots of elevation gain, it is not as tough as the extended version of Hike 10. However, you still need to wear good footwear. Follow the creek bed, staying to the left at the first fork. Continue on until you find a slope on your left that suits your abilities and offers access to the open ridge above. Follow this vegetated ridge to the top — a fantastic viewpoint for the Great Spur, an excellent example of an entrenched river meander [45]. There was a large group of Dall's sheep in the area the last time I was up there.

*Right: Highest point of the ridge, looking towards Deadmen Valley.
Photo: Mary Enright*

Bottom: The Great Spur of the South Nahanni seen from the top of the ridge.

Deadmen Valley.

Leaving Deadmen Valley for First Canyon. Dry Canyon Creek to left.

Deadmen Valley to Kraus Hotsprings

**map
20**

Approximate distances

Deadmen Valley campground to Dry Canyon Creek 4 km
Dry Canyon Creek to George's Riffle 3 km
George's Riffle to Whitespray Spring 19 km
Whitespray Spring to Lafferty Creek 4 km
Lafferty Creek to Lafferty's Riffle 0.5 km
Lafferty's Riffle to Kraus Hotsprings 3.5 km

Total approximate distance 34 km

Don't hurry this interesting section through First Canyon; it's only a short day to Kraus Hotsprings.

When you finally tear yourself away from fascinating Deadmen Valley, you enter First Canyon below Dry Canyon Creek. Here the river cuts through Nahanni Plateau, creating the most dramatic canyon in Canada, its sheer walls rising straight from the river's edge. While your partner manoeuvres the canoe, lie back and watch the fantastic scenes drifting by. There are, however, two rapids to be aware of, the first of which is George's Riffle.

Deadmen Valley Sheep Lick [60] (map 20)

There are several mineral licks located throughout Nahanni, two of which are easily viewed by paddlers. One is located just downstream from the Sunblood warden patrol cabin on river left and the other is located in Deadmen Valley area on river left just downstream from Dry Canyon Creek. Keep your camera ready in case you spot some Dall's sheep, but please don't disturb these animals; take pictures from your boat or from the opposite bank. Dall's sheep depend on minerals from these licks for an important part of their diet and they may become unhealthy if continually frightened away, especially the lambs.

George's Riffle

George's Riffle, also known as Cache Rapids, is your entrance exam into First Canyon. The rapid is located just after the river bends to the left beyond Dry Canyon Creek. Before you reach the rapid, the river picks up speed as it passes through a long riffle section. The rapid is very straightforward, the only hazard being large standing waves. The largest waves extend from river right to mid-channel. The left side is much calmer, so the safest route through is to hug the left side of the main channel which is the right side of the island. As you reach the end of the island, paddle across the mouth of the channel by front ferry, then stay to the left side of the river through the calmer water. At higher water levels you can try paddling down the left side of the island and eddying out where the channel meets the main part of the river. At all water levels I have never experienced any problem with running this rapid by paddling slightly left of centre. This rapid becomes less violent at lower water levels.

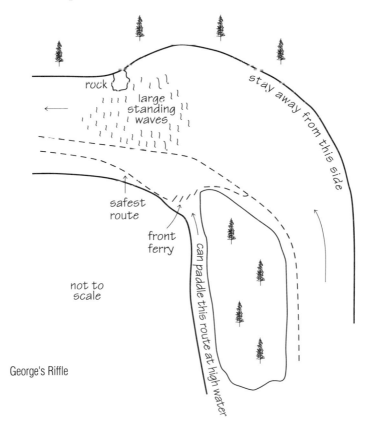

Opposite top: First Canyon, with George's Riffle in the foreground. Photo taken from the island.
Opposite bottom: George's Riffle.

Whitespray Spring.

I've camped at Whitespray Spring where there is room for a couple of tents. Although you don't get the morning sun, the water is fresh — the best in the World. The spring drains the world renowned karstlands located several kilometres to the north.

As you round the next bend, look high up the canyon wall to the left to spot the entrances to Grotte Valerie and other caves.

Lafferty Creek has another camping site and is the start of a hike onto Nahanni Plateau and ultimately to the karstlands.

Lafferty's Riffle

Lafferty's Riffle is even more straightforward than George's. River right gives you the roller-coaster ride, while river left misses it all. If you do run the rapid, be wary of getting too close to the canyon wall where there are some nasty hydraulics. This rapid is created by debris washed down from Lafferty Creek. Consequently, lower water levels produce larger waves, which is in direct contrast to the other rapids on the South Nahanni.

Kraus Hotsprings is located on river right just beyond where the canyon walls drop into low elevation forest. Don't forget to sign in at the last check-in station which is Gus and Mary Kraus's old generator shack. Some paddlers prefer to settle for the night at the top of The Splits after a soak in the springs.

Grotte Valerie [57] (map 20)

Grotte Valerie is the most famous of Nahanni's caves which number over 200 in this area alone. Located in the wall of First Canyon just up-river from Lafferty Creek, it boasts 2 kilometres of passages and caverns. These tunnels formed as water drained downward from sinkholes on the plateau, creating four separate passages — Stalactite Gallery, Ice Lake, Dead Sheep Passage, and the Crystal Passage — which over time, became linked into a single large system.

Public access to the main cave is blocked by a locked gate in an effort to protect the delicate features inside. Actually, it's illegal to enter a cave in any Canadian national park without permission of the park superintendent.

Grotte Valerie has several interesting features and it is a pity public access must be restricted in order to preserve them.

The Stalactite Gallery, for example, contains hundreds of stalactites and a few stalagmites dating back over 350,000 years. Stalactites look somewhat like icicles hanging from the roof of a cave, but are made of minerals. Stalagmites, on the other hand, grow upward from the ground.

Ice Lake provides a very cold obstacle during summer explorations when meltwater collects on top of an extensive sheet of ice.

Dead Sheep Passage contains well-preserved skeletons of more than a hundred Dall's sheep, some over 2,000 years old. It is not uncommon for sheep to seek refuge from a storm in a cave, although it does seem unusual that these sheep wandered in the dark for hundreds of metres before they slid blindly over a small icefall. Unable to scramble back up, they subsequently died.

The Great Ice Passage or *Crystal Passage*, as I prefer to call it, best exemplifies the well-defined microclimatic zonation present in Grotte Valerie. This type of feature is rarely as well developed in caves as it is here. As warm, moist air is drawn down into the cave's depths, the moisture condenses into large feathery ice crystals that cling to the floor, walls and ceiling. Crystals glittering in the beam of a cave lamp make this passage truly spectacular.

Photos overleaf:
page 90: First Canyon. Cliff in the vicinity of Grotte Valerie.
page 91 top: Grotte Valerie, the Great Ice Passage.
page 91 bottom: A long-term resident of Dead Sheep Passage.

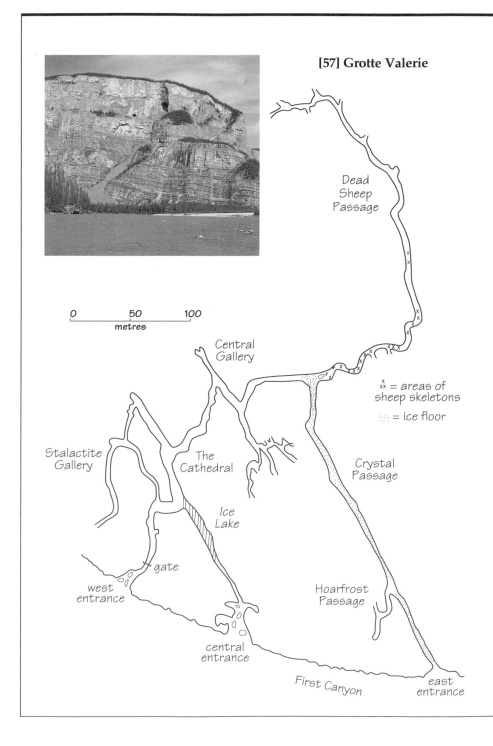

[57] Grotte Valerie

Dead
Sheep
Passage

0   50   100
metres

Central
Gallery

x
xx = areas of
sheep skeletons

= ice floor

Stalactite
Gallery

The
Cathedral

Crystal
Passage

Ice
Lake

gate

west
entrance

Hoarfrost
Passage

central
entrance

First Canyon

east
entrance

Hike 12 Prairie Creek Canyon and Fan (map 20)

The Prairie Creek fan [42] offers easy strolling on flat terrain and gives you the chance to work some of the kinks out of your legs after a day of paddling. More ambitious hikers can follow the stream to the mouth of Prairie Creek Canyon and then carry on into the canyon itself. If the stream is running too strongly or you just don't want to get wet, look for a trail immediately to the left (west) of the canyon mouth. It traverses a low-lying hill, actually an old silt plug [43], and delivers you into a most impressive canyon, every bit as impressive as First Canyon. At the stream source is Cadilac Mine which is no longer in operation.

One of my fondest Nahanni memories is of the antics involved when a group of us lined our canoes up to the canyon and then raced them back to the river. Give it a try!

Spectacular Prairie Creek beyond the silt plug.

Hike 13 Tlogotsho Plateau (map 20)

This is a 20 kilometre return overnight hike requiring appropriate camping equipment and a plentiful supply of water. Start by trekking up Sheaf Creek to the point where it disappears into the plateau, then head to the right, or west, up a steep ridge and cliff to a final elevation of approximately 1550 metres. This is a fairly strenuous hike (10 hours in, 8 out) with several creek crossings and scrambles over deadfall to contend with. The effort is worth it when you sit on the ancient shores of Glacial Lake Nahanni and Tetcela and enjoy the awesome views of Deadmen Valley far below. The plateau is fascinating in its own right [10, 27, 52], but especially in light of recent archaeological discoveries [78] described on page 203.

Right top:
En route to Tlogotsho Plateau.
Photo: Doug Eastcott

Bottom: The flat top
of Tlogotsho Plateau.

Hike 14 Dry Canyon Creek Canyon (map 20)

The canyon of Dry Canyon Creek is an easy hike at first, gradually becoming more difficult as you approach the end of the canyon 10 kilometres distant (rock scrambling up dried-up waterfalls). Footwear with good stiff soles will help offset the discomfort of hiking on small rounded rocks. As with most of the small canyons, there are beautiful fluvial landforms and fossils to view along the way. Watch for Dall's sheep that use a cave located on the wall to the left near the entrance to the canyon.

After hiking into the canyon for some distance the canyon walls yield and allow access onto the Nahanni Plateau. If you get this far consider it an overnight hike so bring the necessary gear. Some hikers use this creek as a northern access to the karstlands, though the topography appears to be quite rough.

A caution: be careful hiking here during potential flash-flood conditions described on page 19. You could be marooned.

photo: Doug Eastcott

Upper Dry Canyon Creek.

Opposite: Lafferty Creek. The river bed at low water showing typical hiking terrain.

Hike 15 Lafferty Creek (map 20)

The hike up Lafferty Creek and canyon is much the same as the one up Dry Canyon Creek (Hike 14). Watch for large, igneous, glacial erratics [17] that were carried 250 kilometres from the Canadian Shield on the back of a long-dead glacier. If you use this creek to gain access to Nahanni Plateau and the karst-lands which lie behind, likely more than one day would be required.

An aerial view of meandering Clausen Creek and the Kraus Hotsprings area.
To left is First Canyon and the deep canyon of Lafferty Creek.

Photo: Doug Eastcott

An aerial view of The Splits.

Kraus Hotsprings to Blackstone Landing

maps
21-24

Approximate distances

Kraus Hotsprings to approximate start of The Splits 20 km
start of The Splits to park boundary 16 km
park boundary to Nahanni Butte 32 km
Nahanni Butte to Blackstone Landing 48 km

Total approximate distance 116 km

The final easy section leaves the Nahanni Plateau behind and enters the western edge of the Mackenzie Plains. It takes a full day to paddle from Kraus Hotsprings to Nahanni Butte and with an additional 6 hours to Blackstone Landing, it would make for a very long day indeed. Plan on staying the night in the Nahanni Butte area.

With the canyons receding in the distance, paddlers pass through the gap in Yohin Ridge into an area of lower gradient known as The Splits. The river continues to move along at a fairly nice pace through this wide open valley, hence there are still areas with currents that warrant caution. Be especially careful of log jams and deadheads which are half-drowned tree trunks sticking up in the water or lying just under the surface. Along the way you pass Yohin Lake, Mattson Mountain and the Sand Blowouts and Twisted Mountain, sometimes climbed for the view. The park boundary roughly corresponds with the end of The Splits, after which the river really slows down through a set of very long, sometimes frustrating meanders. If the wind is favourable you might want to try rigging an impromptu sail.

The Dene village of Nahanni Butte on river right offers a few services such as a campground on the bank, a small store, part-time nursing station, radio telephone and airstrip. Paddlers can de-register at the park office. Across the river from the village lie the deserted remnants of the Nahanni Butte warden station under Nahanni Butte — another good camping spot.

Just downstream of the butte you enter the slow current of the Liard River. A word of caution, if the wind is blowing strong from the east against the current, large standing waves can form from Nahanni Butte to Blackstone, especially in the shallow waters off Swan Point. The entrance of the Blackstone River is quite inconspicuous. Lindberg Landing, however, is obvious since these buildings are the first you encounter at river right after leaving Nahanni Butte. Blackstone Landing campground and visitor centre lie another half kilometre or so beyond in Blackstone Territorial Park.

Kraus Hotsprings [83] (map 21)

Home of the famous slime fights! I used to love flinging the slimy algae growing in the pools at fellow wardens and paddlers who joined in some of the best slime fights ever to hit Nahanni country. The fights usually ended with a cold swim in the river to get cleaned up — great fun!

There are two natural pools and one man-made pool which can be found at riverside (the best slime grows here!). The main spring is about 300 metres south of the river where there are two pools emitting 35°C water. A path at the back of the clearing will take you there. Although the water has all the necessary ingredients for making tufa mounds, the hydrogen-sulphide-rich water creates a weak sulphuric acid which erodes any tufa deposition.

The cabin was the homestead of Gus and Mary Kraus who lived here on and off from 1940 to 1971. In the past other prospector's and adventurer's cabins stood where the old scow now occupies the river bank opposite.

Mud monster at Kraus Hotsprings.

The South Nahanni entering the Mackenzie Plains, showing the tip of Nahnni Butte, the now closed Nahanni Butte warden station and airstrip, and the confluence with the Liard River.

Photo: Mary Enright

Drying out on Swan Point on the Liard River.

99

Yohin Lake (map 21)

One of my best memories of Nahanni involves a magical evening spent exploring the wonders of Yohin Lake. Located in the southeast end of the park, the lake covers 3,200 hectares and includes 222 plant species (19 of which were previously unrecorded) within 22 plant communities. Sixty-five wildlife species actively use the area, including five previously unrecorded species, the most significant of which is the white-rumped sandpiper. Trumpeter swans also use the lake and area as a breeding ground. There are interesting sinkholes on the lake's north shore which provide an important winter refuge for northern pike [59].

Left: Yohin Lake and a Trumpeter swan.

Bottom: Yohin Lake and sinkholes from the air, showing the difficult summer access. Park officials require that you ask for permission to enter this sensitive area.

Sand Blowouts [14] (map 22)

The Sand Blowouts are magnificent wind-sculptured features of highly eroded soft sandstone. Located on the southeast slopes of Mattson Mountain, they consist of a collection of eroded arches, pillars, and spheres resembling flying saucers. Many of these features have a layered appearance caused by ribbons of different coloured sand, and range in colour from gleaming white to purple. When mixed together they look like swirls of raspberry ripple ice cream!

Apparently, some natives once viewed this feature with superstition and referred to it as the Devil's Kitchen.

The Blowouts are almost impossible to get to by land since it would take a supreme effort to bushwhack through the dense willow swamps.

Photo: Doug Eastcott

Hikes 16a & 16b Nahanni Butte (map 23)

If you have the time and inclination, the hike up Nahanni Butte, elevation 1396 m, affords a sweeping vista of The Splits and the massive Mackenzie Plains. A fire tower at the summit is still manned during the summer I believe. Perhaps, with the right approach, you could get a tour.

Hike 16a refers to the route that starts from the bottom of the south ridge where it descends to the river. After gaining the first level spot at the shoulder look around for indications of a trail that leads through the bush to open subalpine terrain. Once in the open, follow the height of land along broken rock to the top. Good footwear, plenty of water, and an ample supply of bug dope are essential.

Another possible route for the more adventurous involves the use of "Peter's Trail" (Hike 16b), that ex-residents of the "park" side of Nahanni Butte built in an effort to keep in shape and to provide an alternative route to the mountain. I've never taken this route all the way to the ridge, but the last known terminus of the trail should leave a hiker within striking distance of the mountain. From the end of the trail I would head for the broken rock/talus slope which provide access to the summit ridge, then follow the easy ridge to the top. As with Hike 16a, you'll need good footwear and plenty of water. Also, because the lower portion lies in forest where there isn't enough wind to blow away the mosquitos, good bug dope is absolutely necessary if you don't want to be eaten alive.

Nahanni Butte from near the old warden cabin.

Flat River: Seaplane Lake to South Nahanni

maps 25-28

Approximate distances

Seaplane Lake to Cascade-of-the-Thirteen-Steps 24 km
Cascade-of-the-Thirteen-Steps to Irvine Creek 19 km
Irvine Creek to South Nahanni River 85 km

Total approximate distance 128 km

I have never paddled the Flat River, although I have patrolled the river up to Irvine Creek by jetboat. The information I provide here comes from a Flat River Touring Guide compiled by Nahanni National Park staff. Although the river is 280 kilometres long, I only describe the 128-kilometre section from Seaplane Lake to the confluence with the South Nahanni which takes about 4-5 days and is a nice escape from the more popular waterways..

The usual landing spot is at a dock located at the big island in Seaplane Lake. There is a camping area on the island. At the extreme northwest end of the lake a well-marked half-kilometre portage trail leads to the river.

The Flat River between here and Irvine Creek has a gradient of 3.2 m/km, and is considered class III overall, providing the Cascade-of-the-Thirteen-Steps Rapid is portaged. In all there are five class III rapids, 18 class II rapids, and 10 class 1 rapids. For the most part, the rapids require enhanced maneuvering capabilities to avoid rocks.

The Cascade-of-the-Thirteen-Steps

The Cascade-of-the-Thirteen-Steps is a 1.2 kilometre-long stretch of class IV-V rapids with large standing waves, many rocks. and several ledges, some of which are over 1.5 metres high. An easily-seen sign on river left indicates the start of the 850 metre-long portage trail. Getting to it can be quite tricky in high water levels. Immediately before the trail you navigate two class II rapids. Below the second rapid the river makes a sharp bend to the right. This is where canoes must eddy out on river left into a small bay about 10 metres upstream of the bend. If you miss this opportunity get ready for a heck of a ride!

Past Irvine Creek (good campsite), the river gradient is reduced to 1.8 m/km and is considered class I overall, although there is a possibility of encountering log jams and sweepers. On river left, just before entering the South Nahanni is the Flat River warden cabin which is patrolled on a regular basis.

Cascade-of-the-Thirteen-Steps from the air. The line of the portage is clearly visible as it zig-zags up the bank at river left and cuts straight across the promontory to the river beyond the rapid. The put in point is opposite a small island.   This is where Frank and Willie McLeod were swamped after returning from a panning trip up Bennett Creek in 1904. All the gold was lost in the rapids! Photo: Canadian Parks Service

Wildmint Hotsprings [81] (map 25)

Wildmint Hotsprings is located alongside the Flat River just within the boundaries of the park. Here a number of bubbling springs flow from the side of a shallow hill. Tufa deposition has formed walls which help maintain three pools, the largest being 2 to 3 metres deep, 75 metres long, and 30 metres wide. On a hot summer day the water within the pools is about 29°C. Unlike Rabbitkettle Hotsprings, the deposition here did not create mound structures. The surrounding area is very lush, with a wide variety of vegetation living in and around the pools, and consequently this attracts a number of wildlife species, including moose which venture into the pools to feed on aquatic plants. Remnants of an old sod-roofed cabin nearby suggest that sometime in the past someone must have lived here.

Top: Tufa walls.
Photo: Doug Eastcott

Bottom: One of the pools
at Wildmint Hotsprings.
Photo: Canadian Parks Service

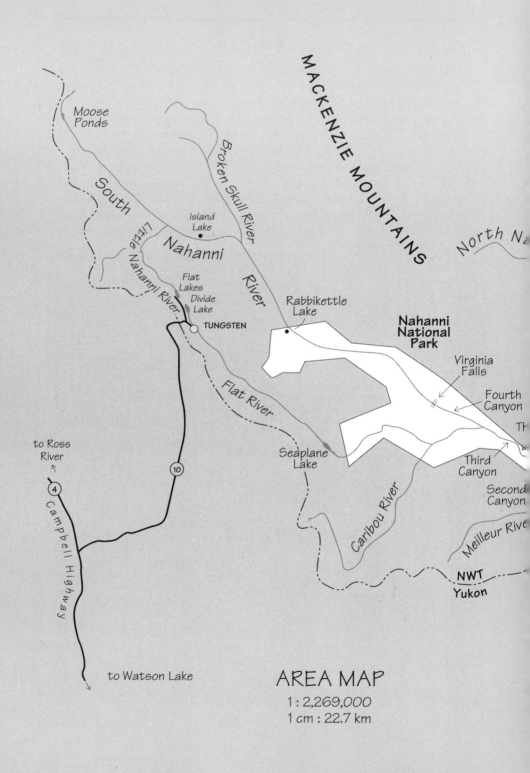

MACKENZIE MOUNTAINS

Moose
Ponds

Broken Skull River

South

Little

Nahanni

Island
Lake

Nahanni River

Flat
Lakes
Divide
Lake

River

North Na

Rabbikettle
Lake

**Nahanni
National
Park**

Virginia
Falls

Fourth
Canyon

Th

TUNGSTEN

Flat River

Seaplane
Lake

Third
Canyon

Second
Canyon

to Ross
River

10

Caribou River

Meilleur Rive

4

NWT
Yukon

Campbell Highway

to Watson Lake

AREA MAP
1 : 2,269,000
1 cm : 22.7 km

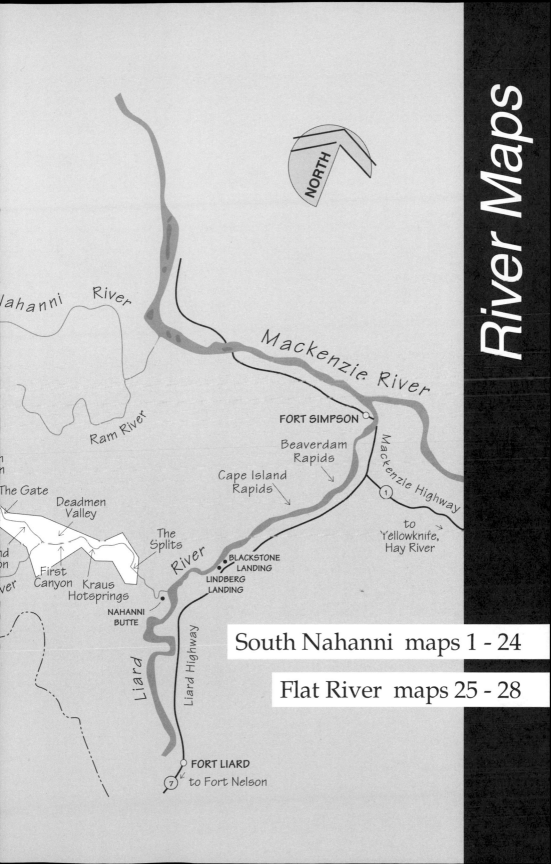

River Maps

NORTH

lahanni River

Mackenzie River

Ram River

FORT SIMPSON

Beaverdam Rapids

Cape Island Rapids

Mackenzie Highway

(1)

to Yellowknife, Hay River

The Gate

Deadmen Valley

The Splits

First Canyon

Kraus Hotsprings

River

BLACKSTONE LANDING

LINDBERG LANDING

NAHANNI BUTTE

Liard

Liard Highway

South Nahanni maps 1 - 24

Flat River maps 25 - 28

FORT LIARD

(7) to Fort Nelson

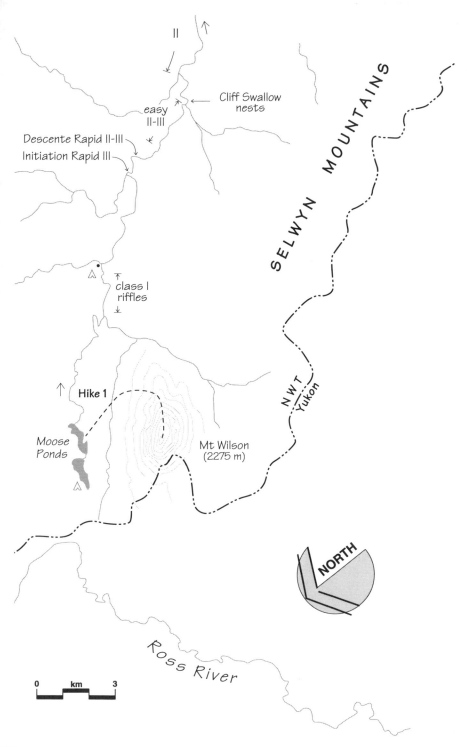

1

South Nahanni : Moose Ponds

II

Cliff Swallow
nests

easy
II-III

Descente Rapid II-III
Initiation Rapid III

class I
riffles

Hike 1

Moose
Ponds

Mt Wilson
(2275 m)

SELWYN MOUNTAINS

N W T
Yukon

NORTH

Ross River

0   km   3

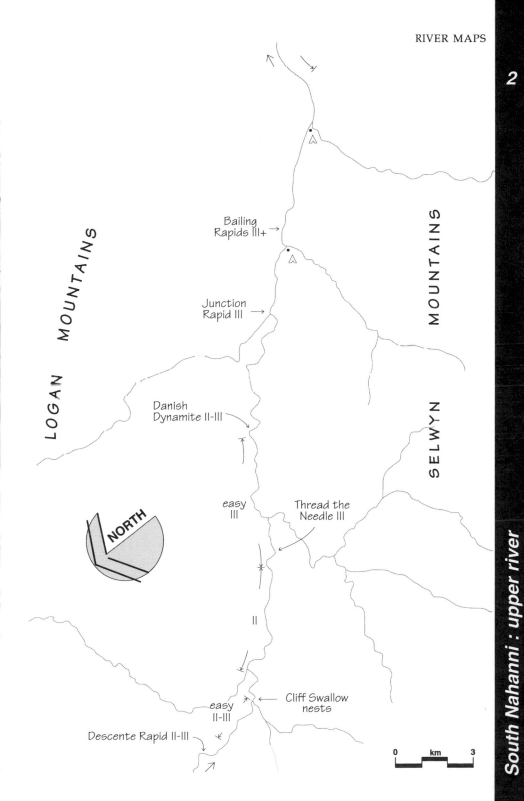

LOGAN MOUNTAINS

SELWYN MOUNTAINS

Bailing
Rapids III+ →

Junction
Rapid III →

Danish
Dynamite II-III

easy
III

Thread the
Needle III

II

easy
II-III

Cliff Swallow
nests

Descente Rapid II-III

NORTH

0   km   3

South Nahanni : upper river

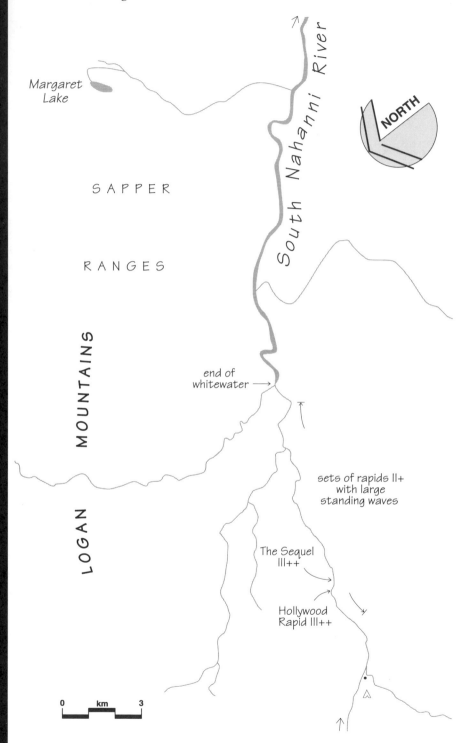

Margaret
Lake

S A P P E R

R A N G E S

M O U N T A I N S

L O G A N

South Nahanni River

NORTH

end of
whitewater ⟶

sets of rapids II+
with large
standing waves

The Sequel
III++

Hollywood
Rapid III++

0   km   3

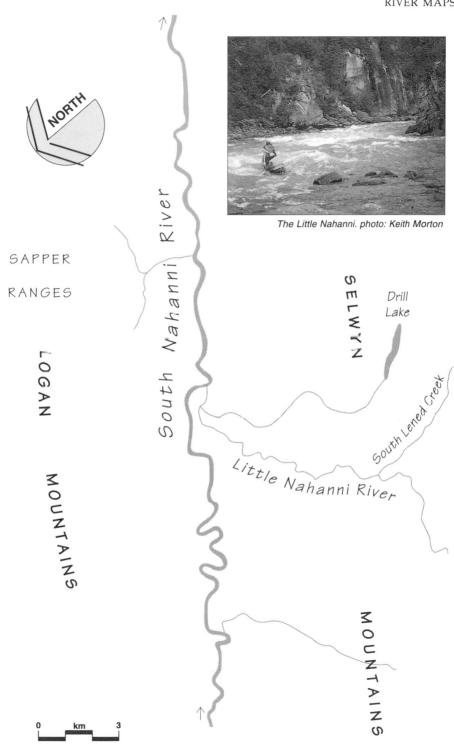

NORTH

The Little Nahanni. photo: Keith Morton

SAPPER

RANGES

South Nahanni River

LOGAN

MOUNTAINS

SELWYN

Drill Lake

South Lened Creek

Little Nahanni River

MOUNTAINS

0 km 3

South Nahanni : Little Nahanni River confluence

111

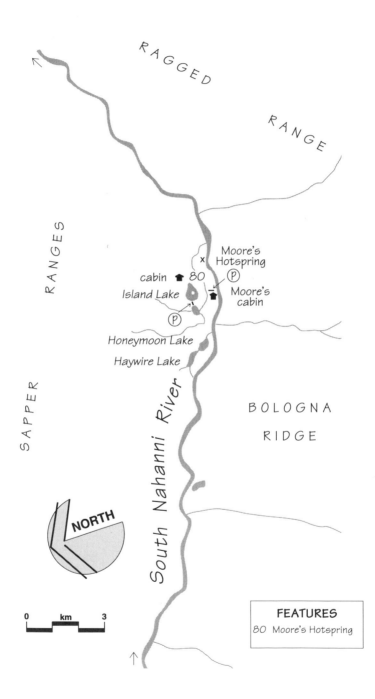

FEATURES

80 Moore's Hotspring

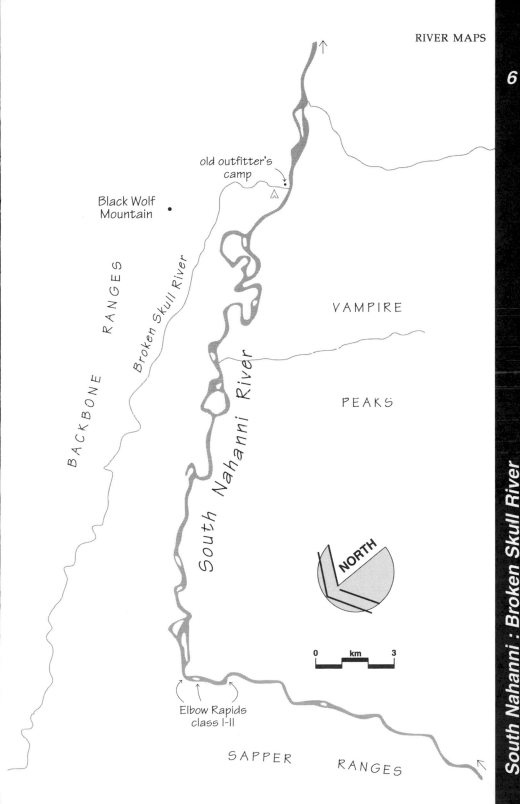

old outfitter's camp

Black Wolf Mountain

B A C K B O N E   R A N G E S

Broken Skull River

South Nahanni River

V A M P I R E

P E A K S

NORTH

0   km   3

Elbow Rapids
class I-II

S A P P E R   R A N G E S

South Nahanni : Broken Skull River

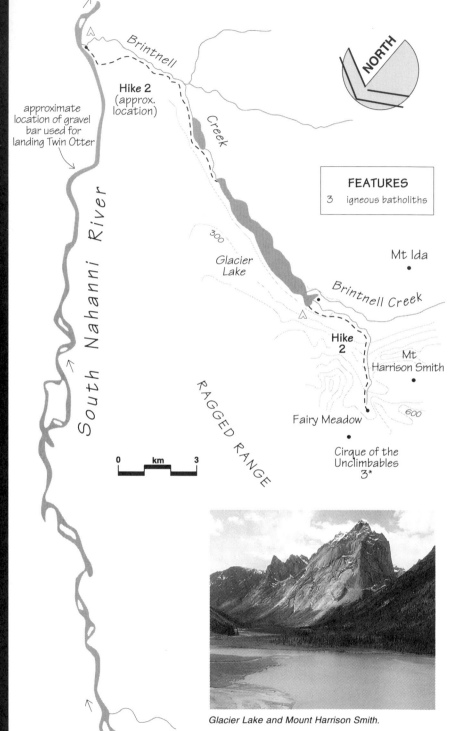

approximate
location of gravel
bar used for
landing Twin Otter

Brintnell

Hike 2
(approx.
location)

Creek

NORTH

FEATURES

3   igneous batholiths

South Nahanni River

300

Glacier
Lake

Mt Ida

Brintnell Creek

Hike
2

Mt
Harrison Smith

RAGGED RANGE

600

Fairy Meadow

Cirque of the
Unclimbables
3*

0   km   3

Glacier Lake and Mount Harrison Smith.

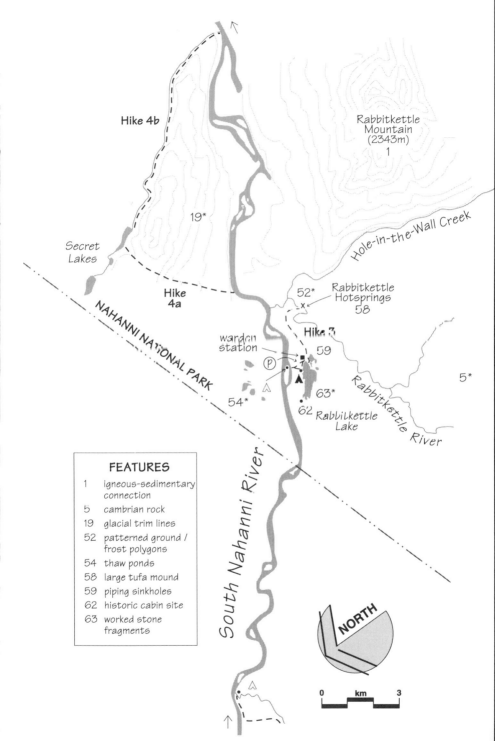

Hike 4b

Rabbitkettle
Mountain
(2343m)
1

19*

Hole-in-the-Wall Creek

Secret
Lakes

Hike
4a

52*
x

Rabbitkettle
Hotsprings
58

Hike 3

NAHANNI NATIONAL PARK

warden
station

(P)

59

5*

54*

63*

62 Rabbitkettle
Lake

Rabbitkettle River

South Nahanni River

FEATURES

1   igneous-sedimentary
    connection
5   cambrian rock
19 glacial trim lines
52 patterned ground /
    frost polygons
54 thaw ponds
58 large tufa mound
59 piping sinkholes
62 historic cabin site
63 worked stone
    fragments

NORTH

0   km   3

Nahanni: the river guide

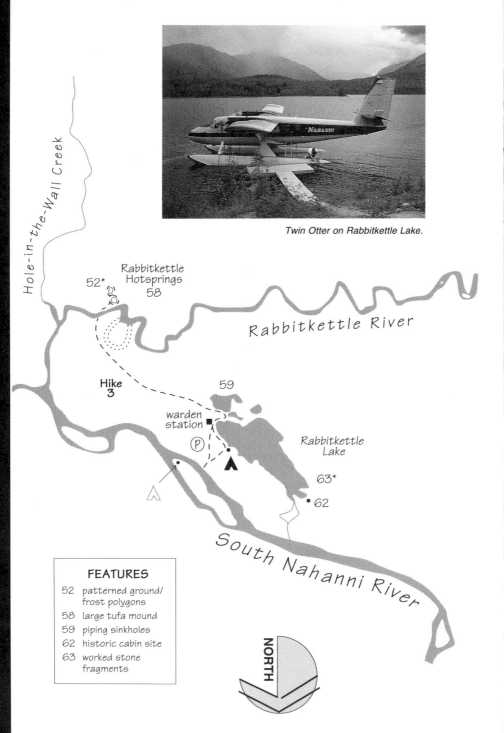

Twin Otter on Rabbitkettle Lake.

FEATURES

52 patterned ground/
    frost polygons
58 large tufa mound
59 piping sinkholes
62 historic cabin site
63 worked stone
    fragments

NORTH

South Nahanni : Rabbitkettle detail

9

Map labels:

Hole-in-the-Wall Creek

52*

Rabbitkettle
Hotsprings
58

Rabbitkettle River

Hike
3

59

warden
station

(p)

Rabbitkettle
Lake

63*

62

South Nahanni River

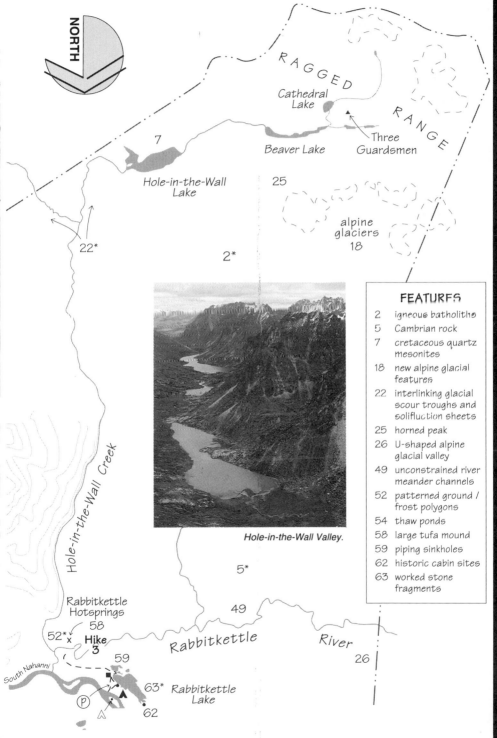

NORTH

RAGGED

Cathedral
Lake

RANGE

Three
Guardsmen

7

Beaver Lake

Hole-in-the-Wall
Lake

25

alpine
glaciers
18

22*

2*

Hole-in-the-Wall Valley.

5*

Hole-in-the-Wall Creek

Rabbitkettle
Hotsprings
58
52* x   **Hike**
3

South Nahanni

59

Rabbitkettle

River

49

26

63*   Rabbitkettle
Lake

62

P

FEATURES

2	igneous batholiths
5	Cambrian rock
7	cretaceous quartz mesonites
18	new alpine glacial features
22	interlinking glacial scour troughs and solifluction sheets
25	horned peak
26	U-shaped alpine glacial valley
49	unconstrained river meander channels
52	patterned ground / frost polygons
54	thaw ponds
58	large tufa mound
59	piping sinkholes
62	historic cabin sites
63	worked stone fragments

South Nahanni : Hole-in-the-Wall detail

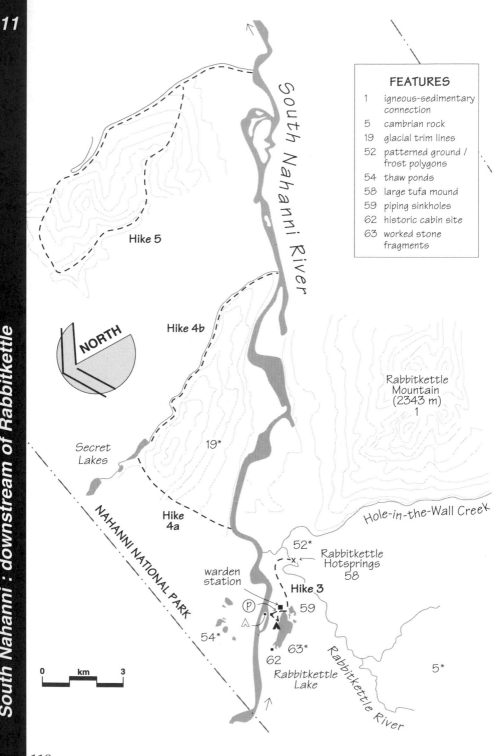

FEATURES

1	igneous-sedimentary connection
5	cambrian rock
19	glacial trim lines
52	patterned ground / frost polygons
54	thaw ponds
58	large tufa mound
59	piping sinkholes
62	historic cabin site
63	worked stone fragments

South Nahanni River

Hike 5

NORTH

Hike 4b

Rabbitkettle
Mountain
(2343 m)
1

Secret
Lakes

19*

Hole-in-the-Wall Creek

Hike
4a

NAHANNI NATIONAL PARK

52*
x
Rabbitkettle
Hotsprings
58

warden
station

Hike 3

P
59
A

54*

63*

62

5*

Rabbitkettle
Lake

Rabbitkettle River

0   km   3

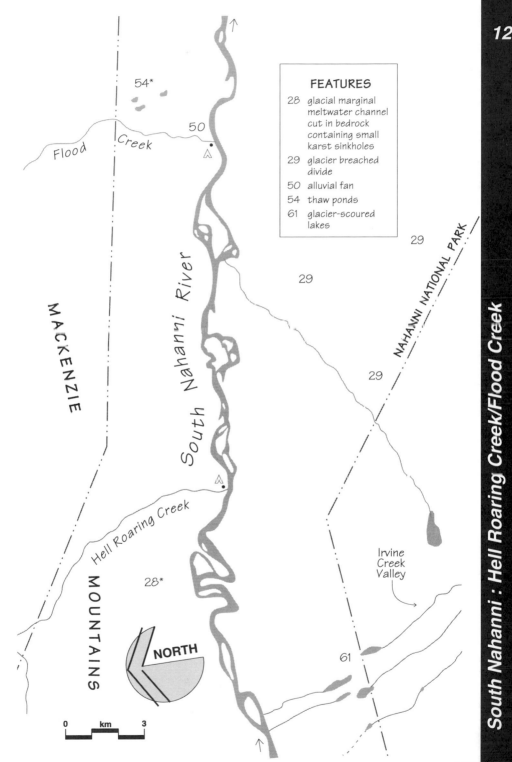

FEATURES

28 glacial marginal meltwater channel cut in bedrock containing small karst sinkholes
29 glacier breached divide
50 alluvial fan
54 thaw ponds
61 glacier-scoured lakes

South Nahanni : Hell Roaring Creek/Flood Creek

13

South Nahanni : Flood Creek to Sunblood

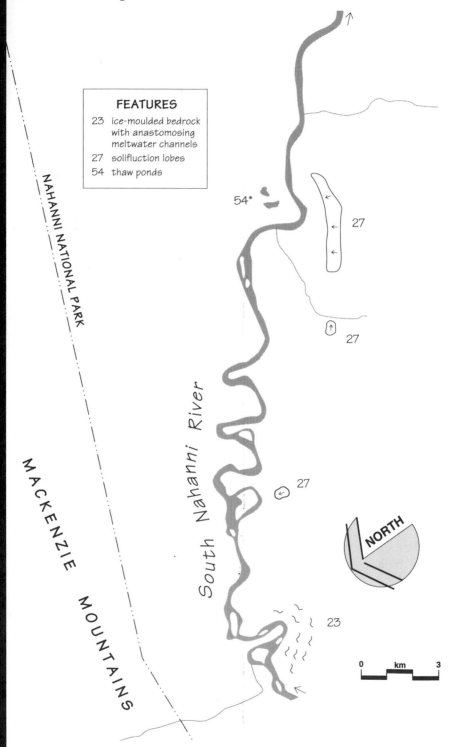

FEATURES

23 ice-moulded bedrock
    with anastomosing
    meltwater channels

27 solifluction lobes

54 thaw ponds

NAHANNI NATIONAL PARK

MACKENZIE MOUNTAINS

South Nahanni River

54*

27

27

27

23

NORTH

0   km   3

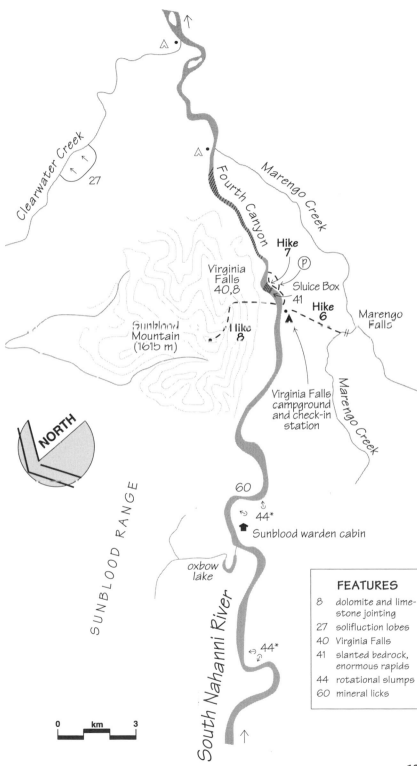

Clearwater Creek

27

Fourth Canyon

Marengo Creek

Hike
7

ⓟ

Virginia
Falls
40,8

Sluice Box

41

Hike
6

Marengo
Falls

Sunblood
Mountain
(1615 m)

Hike
8

Virginia Falls
campground
and check-in
station

Marengo Creek

NORTH

SUNBLOOD RANGE

60

44*

Sunblood warden cabin

oxbow
lake

South Nahanni River

44*

FEATURES

8	dolomite and lime-stone jointing
27	solifluction lobes
40	Virginia Falls
41	slanted bedrock, enormous rapids
44	rotational slumps
60	mineral licks

0 km 3

South Nahanni : Sunblood to Virginia Falls

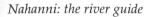

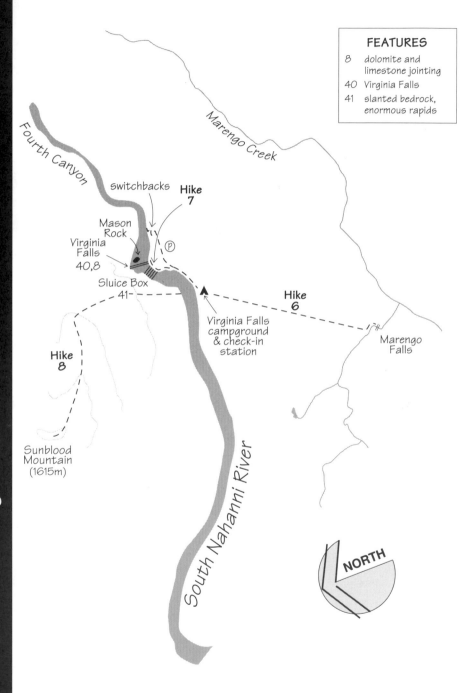

FEATURES

8 dolomite and limestone jointing
40 Virginia Falls
41 slanted bedrock, enormous rapids

Marengo Creek

Fourth Canyon

switchbacks   **Hike 7**

Mason Rock

Virginia Falls
40,8

Sluice Box
41

Ⓟ

Virginia Falls campground & check-in station

Hike 6

Marengo Falls

Hike 8

Sunblood Mountain (1615m)

South Nahanni River

NORTH

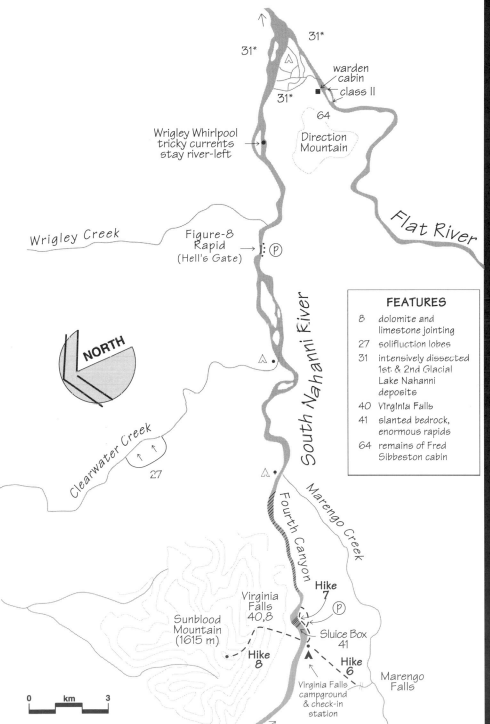

31*

31*

31*

warden
cabin
class II

64
Direction
Mountain

Wrigley Whirlpool
tricky currents
stay river-left →

Flat River

Wrigley Creek

Figure-8
Rapid →
(Hell's Gate)

P

NORTH

South Nahanni River

Clearwater Creek

27

FEATURES

8	dolomite and limestone jointing
27	solifluction lobes
31	intensively dissected 1st & 2nd Glacial Lake Nahanni deposits
40	Virginia Falls
41	slanted bedrock, enormous rapids
64	remains of Fred Sibbeston cabin

Fourth Canyon

Marengo Creek

Hike
7

P

Virginia
Falls
40,8

Sunblood
Mountain
(1615 m)

Sluice Box
41

Hike
8

Hike
6

Marengo
Falls

Virginia Falls
campground
& check-in
station

0   km   3

123

South Nahanni : Virginia Falls to Flat River

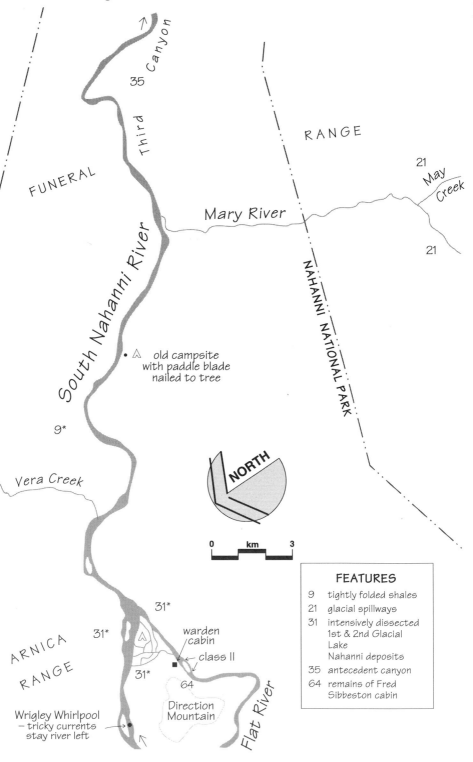

South Nahanni : Flat River to Third Canyon

old campsite
with paddle blade
nailed to tree

9*

Vera Creek

31*

31*   warden
            cabin

31*   ← class II

64

Direction
Mountain

Wrigley Whirlpool
– tricky currents
stay river left

ARNICA

RANGE

FUNERAL

Third Canyon

35

South Nahanni River

Mary River

RANGE

21
May
Creek

21

NAHANNI NATIONAL PARK

NORTH

0   km   3

Flat River

FEATURES

9	tightly folded shales
21	glacial spillways
31	intensively dissected 1st & 2nd Glacial Lake Nahanni deposits
35	antecedent canyon
64	remains of Fred Sibbeston cabin

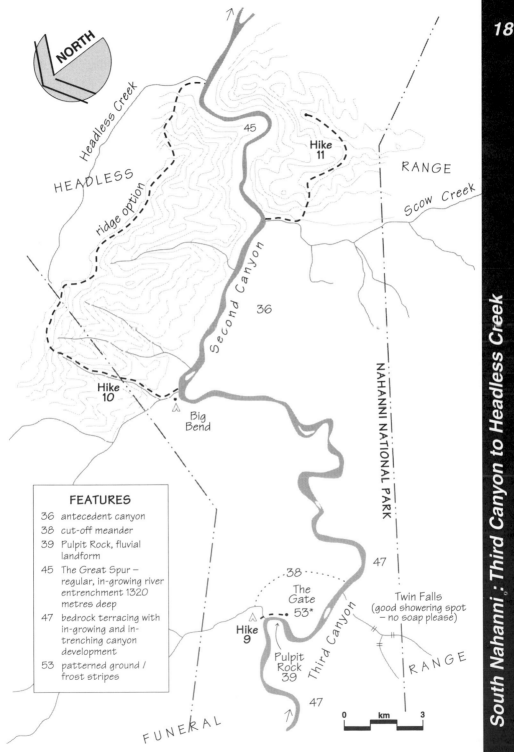

NORTH

Headless Creek

HEADLESS

ridge option

45

Hike
11

RANGE

Scow Creek

Second Canyon

36

Hike
10

Big
Bend

NAHANNI NATIONAL PARK

FEATURES

36 antecedent canyon

38 cut-off meander

39 Pulpit Rock, fluvial
    landform

45 The Great Spur –
    regular, in-growing river
    entrenchment 1320
    metres deep

47 bedrock terracing with
    in-growing and in-
    trenching canyon
    development

53 patterned ground /
    frost stripes

38

The
Gate
53*

47

Twin Falls
(good showering spot
– no soap please)

Hike
9

Pulpit
Rock
39

Third Canyon

47

RANGE

FUNERAL

0   km   3

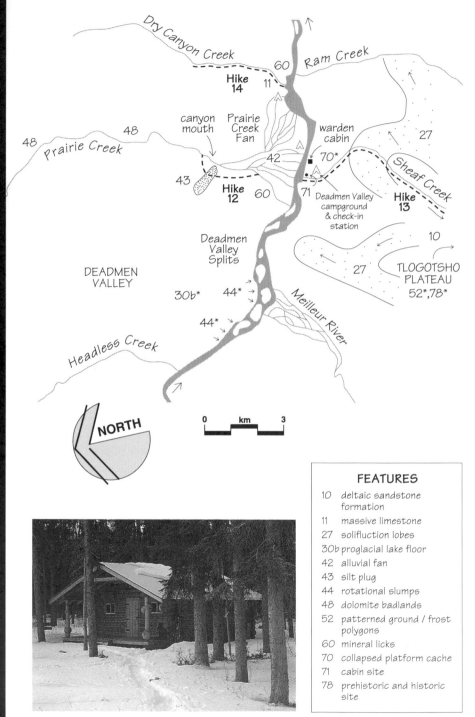

Deadmen Valley warden cabin.

FEATURES

10 deltaic sandstone formation
11 massive limestone
27 solifluction lobes
30b proglacial lake floor
42 alluvial fan
43 silt plug
44 rotational slumps
48 dolomite badlands
52 patterned ground / frost polygons
60 mineral licks
70 collapsed platform cache
71 cabin site
78 prehistoric and historic site

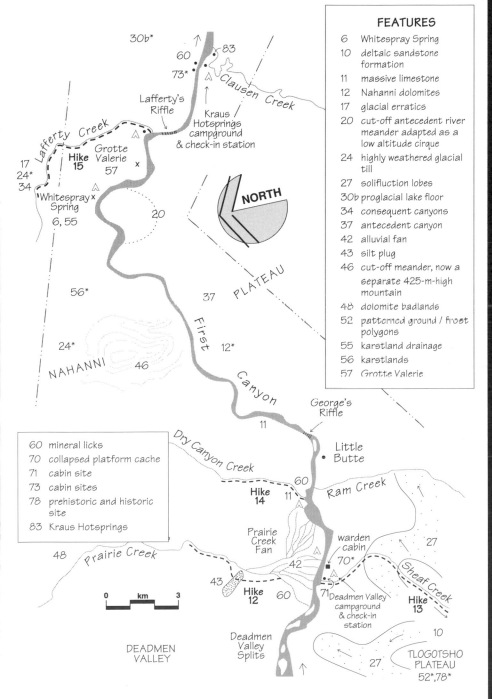

FEATURES

6 Whitespray Spring
10 deltaic sandstone formation
11 massive limestone
12 Nahanni dolomites
17 glacial erratics
20 cut-off antecedent river meander adapted as a low altitude cirque
24 highly weathered glacial till
27 solifluction lobes
30b proglacial lake floor
34 consequent canyons
37 antecedent canyon
42 alluvial fan
43 silt plug
46 cut-off meander, now a separate 425-m-high mountain
48 dolomite badlands
52 patterned ground / frost polygons
55 karstland drainage
56 karstlands
57 Grotte Valerie

60 mineral licks
70 collapsed platform cache
71 cabin site
73 cabin sites
78 prehistoric and historic site
83 Kraus Hotsprings

30b*
60
83
73*
Lafferty's Riffle
Kraus Hotsprings campground & check-in station
Clausen Creek
Lafferty Creek
Grotte Valerie
Hike 15
57
17
24*
34
Whitespray Spring
6, 55
20
NORTH
56*
37
PLATEAU
24*
NAHANNI
46
First Canyon
12*
George's Riffle
11
Dry Canyon Creek
Little Butte
Hike 14
11
60
Ram Creek
27
Prairie Creek Fan
warden cabin
70*
42
Sheaf Creek
48
Prairie Creek
43
Hike 12
60
71
Deadmen Valley campground & check-in station
Hike 13
10
0   km   3
DEADMEN VALLEY
Deadmen Valley Splits
27
TLOGOTSHO PLATEAU
52*,78*

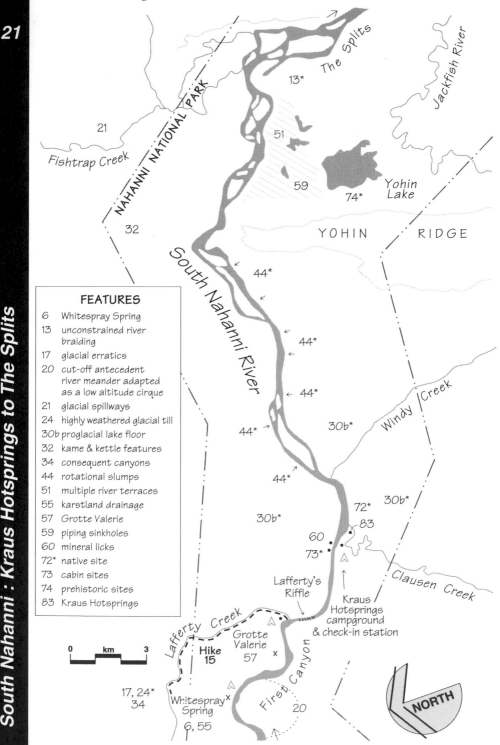

FEATURES

6 Whitespray Spring
13 unconstrained river braiding
17 glacial erratics
20 cut-off antecedent river meander adapted as a low altitude cirque
21 glacial spillways
24 highly weathered glacial till
30b proglacial lake floor
32 kame & kettle features
34 consequent canyons
44 rotational slumps
51 multiple river terraces
55 karstland drainage
57 Grotte Valerie
59 piping sinkholes
60 mineral licks
72* native site
73 cabin sites
74 prehistoric sites
83 Kraus Hotsprings

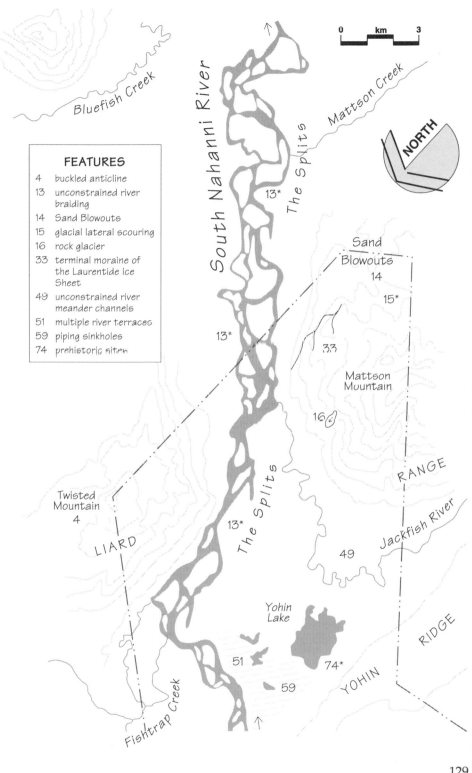

0 — km — 3

NORTH

FEATURES

4   buckled anticline
13 unconstrained river braiding
14 Sand Blowouts
15 glacial lateral scouring
16 rock glacier
33 terminal moraine of the Laurentide Ice Sheet
49 unconstrained river meander channels
51 multiple river terraces
59 piping sinkholes
74 prehistoric sites

Bluefish Creek

South Nahanni River

Mattson Creek

The Splits

13*

Sand Blowouts
14

15*

13*

33

Mattson Mountain

16

RANGE

Twisted Mountain
4

LIARD

The Splits

13*

Jackfish River

49

Yohin Lake

RIDGE

51

74*

YOHIN

59

Fishtrap Creek

South Nahanni : The Splits

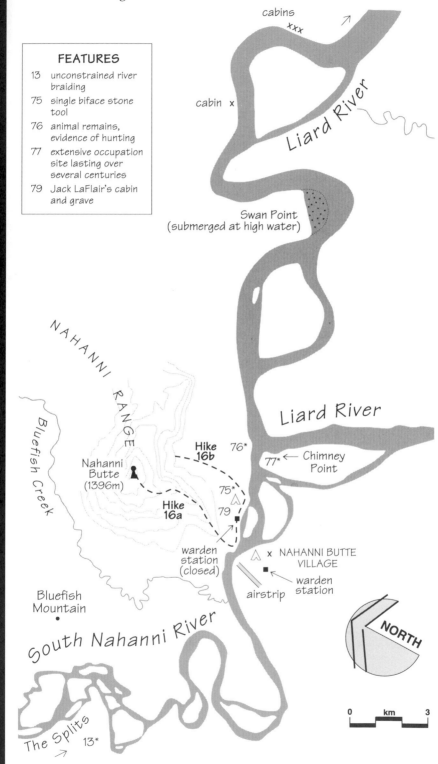

FEATURES

13 unconstrained river
    braiding
75 single biface stone
    tool
76 animal remains,
    evidence of hunting
77 extensive occupation
    site lasting over
    several centuries
79 Jack LaFlair's cabin
    and grave

cabins
xxx

cabin x

Liard River

Swan Point
(submerged at high water)

Liard River

NAHANNI RANGE

Bluefish Creek

Nahanni
Butte
(1396m)

Hike
16b

Hike
16a

76*

77* ← Chimney
        Point

75*

79

warden
station
(closed)

x NAHANNI BUTTE
   VILLAGE

← warden
   station

airstrip

Bluefish
Mountain
•

South Nahanni River

The Splits   13*

NORTH

0   km   3

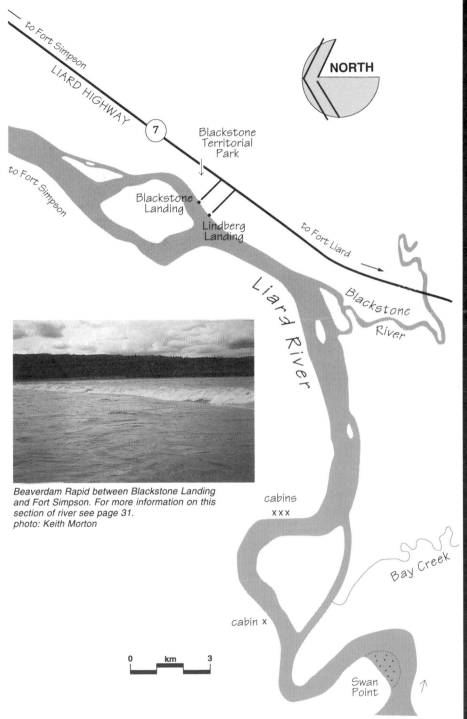

NORTH

to Fort Simpson

LIARD HIGHWAY

⑦

to Fort Simpson

Blackstone
Territorial
Park

Blackstone
Landing

Lindberg
Landing

to Fort Liard →

Liard River

Blackstone
River

*Beaverdam Rapid between Blackstone Landing
and Fort Simpson. For more information on this
section of river see page 31.*
photo: Keith Morton

cabins
x x x

Bay Creek

cabin x

0   km   3

Swan
Point

South Nahanni : Liard River to Blackstone Landing

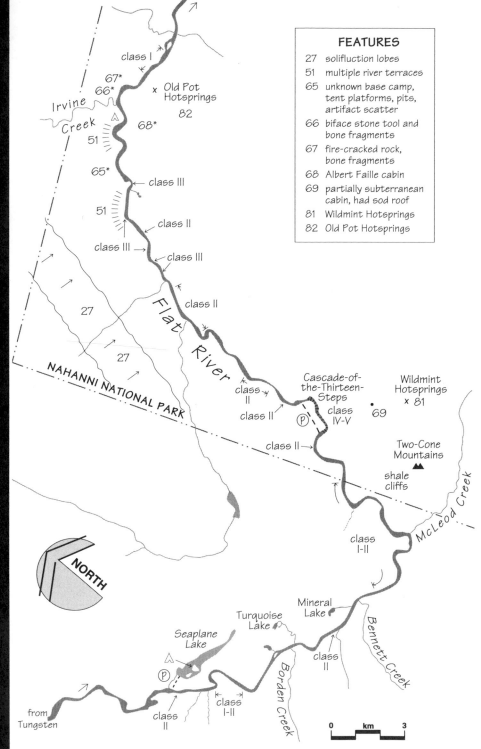

FEATURES

27	solifluction lobes
51	multiple river terraces
65	unknown base camp, tent platforms, pits, artifact scatter
66	biface stone tool and bone fragments
67	fire-cracked rock, bone fragments
68	Albert Faille cabin
69	partially subterranean cabin, had sod roof
81	Wildmint Hotsprings
82	Old Pot Hotsprings

class I

67*
66*

Irvine Creek

Old Pot Hotsprings
82

68*

51

65*

51

class III

class II

class III

class III

class II

27

Flat River

27

NAHANNI NATIONAL PARK

class II

class II

Cascade-of-the-Thirteen-Steps

class IV-V

Wildmint Hotsprings
x 81

69

class II

Two-Cone Mountains

shale cliffs

NORTH

class I-II

McLeod Creek

Mineral Lake

Turquoise Lake

Seaplane Lake

class II

Bennett Creek

Borden Creek

from Tungsten

class II

class I-II

0   km   3

26

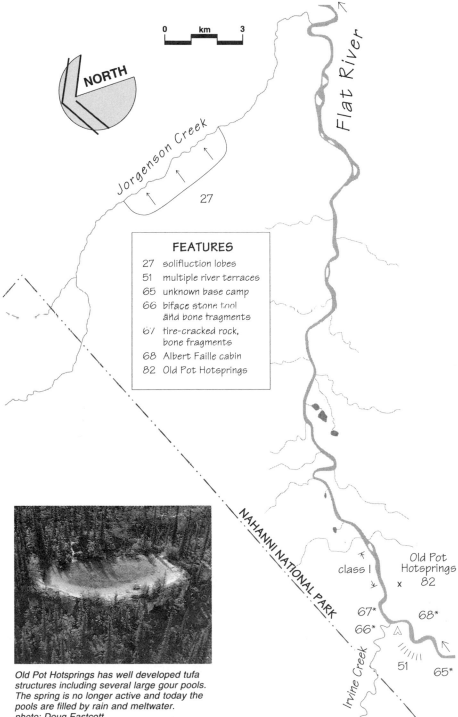

FEATURES

27 solifluction lobes
51 multiple river terraces
65 unknown base camp
66 biface stone tool
    and bone fragments
67 fire-cracked rock,
    bone fragments
68 Albert Faille cabin
82 Old Pot Hotsprings

*Old Pot Hotsprings has well developed tufa
structures including several large gour pools.
The spring is no longer active and today the
pools are filled by rain and meltwater.
photo: Doug Eastcott*

Flat River : Irvine Creek to Jorgenson Creek

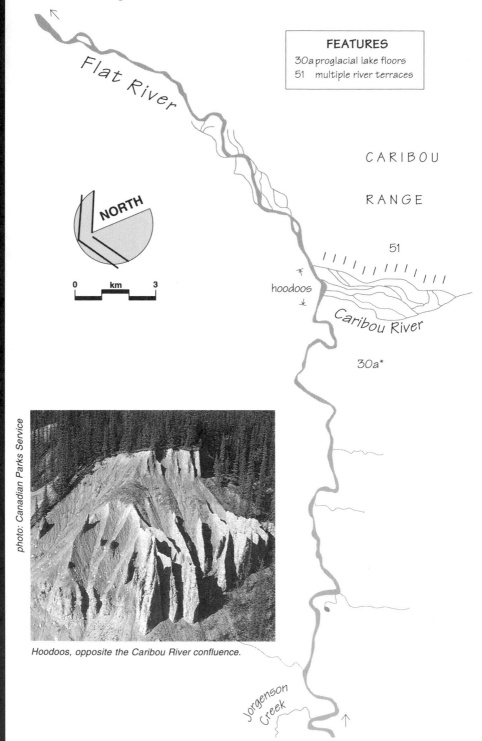

FEATURES
30a proglacial lake floors
51   multiple river terraces

CARIBOU

RANGE

51

hoodoos

Caribou River

30a*

Flat River

NORTH

0   km   3

Jorgenson Creek

photo: Canadian Parks Service

Hoodoos, opposite the Caribou River confluence.

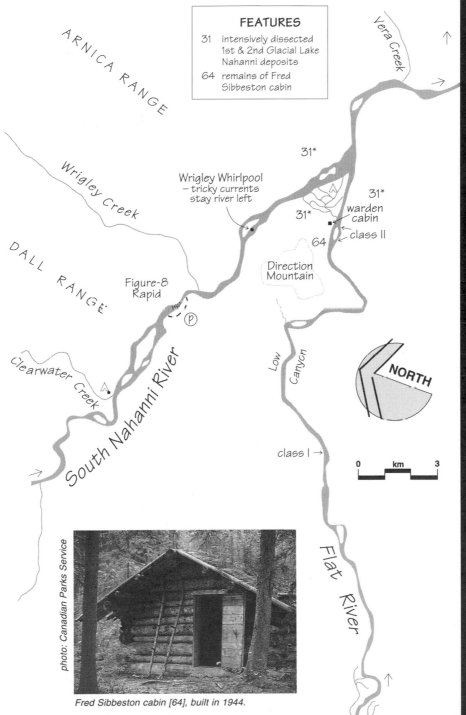

FEATURES

31 intensively dissected
    1st & 2nd Glacial Lake
    Nahanni deposits

64 remains of Fred
    Sibbeston cabin

ARNICA RANGE

Vera Creek

Wrigley Creek

DALL RANGE

Wrigley Whirlpool
– tricky currents
stay river left

31*

31*

31*
warden
cabin

← class II

64

Direction
Mountain

Figure-8
Rapid

Clearwater Creek

South Nahanni River

Low Canyon

class I →

NORTH

0   km   3

Fred Sibbeston cabin [64], built in 1944.

photo: Canadian Parks Service

Flat River

Flat River : South Nahanni confluence

The Nahanni Story

A Unique Landscape

Even during my first trip down the South Nahanni River I couldn't help but notice the tremendous variety of landforms in this majestic country. Indeed, Nahanni has the largest variety of landforms found in any of Canada's national parks. The impetus for establishing a national park in Nahanni came from an enlightened public who demanded protection for some of the area's significant features like Virginia Falls, Rabbitkettle Hotsprings, and the canyon system. Thankfully, these features and many others will endure through time, benefiting the generations to come.

This chapter begins with a discussion of Nahanni's geological history, then expands into a general consideration of the relationship between the geology and geomorphology of the park. Many people confuse geology with geomorphology. This distinction may help: while geologists study rocks, their mineral elements and structure, geomorphologists discuss the processes that gave birth to surrounding landforms. While the subjects are distinct, they have much in common.

Geological History

Three main geological events have shaped the Nahanni basin.

Between 550 and 200 million years ago, the Nahanni region consisted of a continental shelf submerged under a large tropical ocean. Over millions of years the land surrounding this ocean eroded, depositing sand and mud onto the shelf which ultimately, under pressure, became sandstone and shale. This was followed by a period when sediments stopped being deposited. As the skeletons of marine life accumulated, their skeletons provided the carbonate

Previous pages: Second Polje in the karstlands. photo: Doug Eastcott

from which limestone eventually formed. Occasionally, when the calcium component of limestone was replaced with magnesium, the limestone converted to dolomite. The estimated depth of the entire prehistoric sedimentary layer is from 5,600 to 6,800 metres.

Starting about 200 million years ago, mountains began to form as the submarine shelf collided with and very slowly slid over the oceanic plate. This process stopped approximately 100 million years ago, roughly the same time as igneous batholiths (large masses of rock derived from the Earth's core) were injected upwards into that part of the Nahanni now occupied by the Ragged Range.

From two to eight million years ago the continent drifted into the colder latitudes of the northwest. Continental erosion, with its glacial and fluvial (river/stream) erosion, became the dominant force in shaping the landscape you see today. Much of the unconsolidated debris from this erosion still remain in Nahanni's valleys and sometimes approach depths of up to 200 metres.

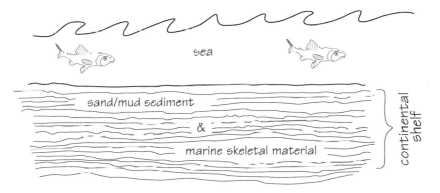

Mineral deposition on the submarine continental shelf of ancient Nahanni.

Nahanni's Geological Regions

There are three significant geological regions within Nahanni National Park. The first occurs at the west end of the park where igneous rocks tower towards the sky. These rocks originated from deep within the earth where two large igneous batholiths were forced toward the earth's surface and were subsequently exposed by the erosion of the overlying sedimentary rock. This can most easily be seen on Rabbitkettle Mountain [1] where lighter-coloured sedimentary rock lies on the lower slopes of the mountain below exposures of darker-coloured igneous rock. The remnants of the two batholiths are located immediately east and west of Hole-in-the-Wall Creek [2*] and form Nahanni's highest and most rugged range of mountains called the Ragged Range. Cirque of the Unclimbables [3*], located just north of the park's northwest boundary, is also part of this batholithic structure.

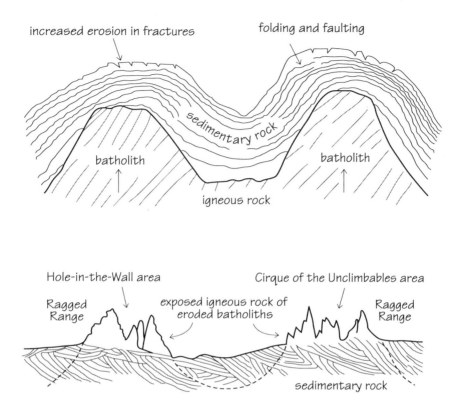

How the Nahanni batholith rocks were formed.

The second region consists of the area from Rabbitkettle River to the east end of Third Canyon. Here, the rocks are considered Lower Paleozoic sedimentaries, roughly 390 million years old. Rocks in this area are folded and faulted from pressures exerted by the igneous injections mentioned in the previous paragraph, and from the mountain-building process.

The third region, from Headless Creek in Second Canyon to Yohin Ridge, consists of deformed Upper Paleozoic sedimentaries, roughly 230 million years old. This area is characterized by three large anticlines and two synclines, these deformed features representing the best examples of large-scale folding found in any Canadian national park. This folding process may still be occurring in First Canyon and in areas located immediately to the east.

Top right:
Twisted Mountain anticline.

Bottom right:
The Ragged Range batholiths. Lotus Flower Tower and Parrot's Beak in the Cirque of the Unclimbables.

Photos: Doug Eastcott

Nahanni – a folded landscape

Rock folds are some of the most obvious geological features you will see along the river, the small-scale synclines and anticlines being relatively easy to spot in the canyon walls. In most cases, the ridges in Nahanni are actually formed by anticlines while the valleys are part of synclines. However, there are instance when the apex of an anticline is so severely deformed by folding that large cracks develop and weaken the structure, thus allowing for more rapid erosion. The resulting landform is one in which the original anticline now forms a depression, or valley, while the more resistant, tightly folded structure of the syncline forms a hill or ridge. This type of landform is often called "inverted topography".

Two specific examples of folding to look for as you paddle down the river are the boat-shaped downfold of Yohin Ridge, which is part of a larger syncline, and the buckled anticline known as Twisted Mountain [4].

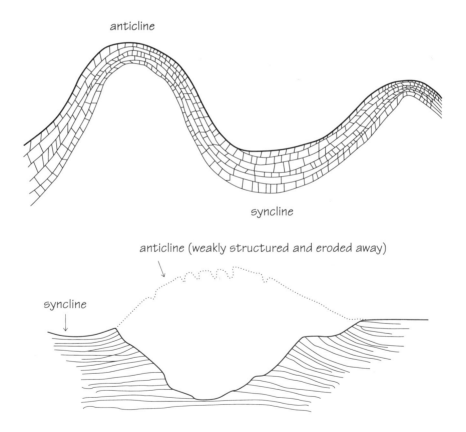

Anticlines and Synclines.

Significant Geological Features of the Nahanni

Dolomite, formed during the Cambrian age, 620 million years ago, is the oldest visible type of rock in the park. It is found in the Rabbitkettle Valley [5*], but is most obvious in First and Second Canyons. You will likely find it hard to distinguish between dolomite and limestone, but generally, from a distance, dolomite appears buff to apricot in colour while limestone looks more grey. Along the Prairie Creek drainage thin dolomites have weathered into a badland type of topography — a rather rare feature for dolomites [48]. Whitespray Spring [6] demonstrates the capacity of dolomite to hold and channel large volumes of water, a role instrumental in the development and maintenance of world-renowned karst features located north of First Canyon [56*]. The walls in the eastern sector of Third Canyon are quite remarkable because they portray well-defined and uniform examples of *all* the major classes of sedimentary rock.

As mentioned previously, granitic rocks are found only in the Ragged Range. These rocks are approximately 110 million years old, or from the Cretacious period, which roughly corresponds with the birth of the Rocky Mountains. These rocks were injected from deep within the earth as magma, eventually cooling and solidifying while still within the earth. Hence, the rock is coarsely crystalline and quite rough, comprised mainly of quartz monzonites and grandiorites. The typical assemblage consists of 15 to 40 percent very large potash feldspar crystals with medium to large crystals of quartz, feldspar, biotite, and hornblende. The granite weathers to a light to medium grey, but from a distance appears dark brown to black due to a lichen covering.

The following features are also considered geologically significant:

- [7] large slabs of cretacious quartz mesonites (S side of Hole-in-the-Wall Lake)
- [8] a good example of sedimentary jointing of massive dolomite and limestone formations (Virginia Falls)
- [9*] tightly folded shales (north bank between Vera Creek and Mary River)
- [10] a massive sandstone formation from an ancient delta (north side of Tlogotsho Plateau)
- [11] the massive limestone of the Nahanni Formation riddled with caverns and rich in fossils (mouth of Dry Canyon Creek and north bank – west end of First Canyon)
- [12*] the layered and multicoloured Nahanni dolomites (First Canyon)

It is interesting to note how little evidence there is of metamorphic rock. Since this type of rock is formed from heat and pressure on previously formed rock, it would logically follow that the injection of igneous rock in the Ragged Range would have created metamorphic rock as well. This does not appear to have happened to any significant extent, except for some areas of shale that were converted into slate in the Rabbitkettle Valley.

The Geology/Landform Relationship

Geologic structure and rock type have played significant roles in the development of landforms.

To get an idea of the influence of rock type just look toward the Ragged Range from Rabbitkettle Lake and notice how the weaker sedimentary rock has eroded faster than the igneous rock. Consequently, the Ragged Range forms the most rugged and highest mountains in Nahanni while the surrounding valley bottoms generally consist of highly eroded shales.

An obvious association between geologic structure and landform is shown by the drainage pattern adopted by a land mass as a result of its bedrock structure.

Here are four examples:

• The igneous batholiths in the northwestern end of the park originally formed as domes made of uniform and erosion-resistant igneous rock. This created a radial drainage pattern as water was shed more or less equally from all sides of the dome.

• East of Irvine Creek the relationship between drainage pattern and geologic structure has been disrupted by glacial erosion. At one time, the upper South Nahanni followed the present Irvine Creek drainage down to Borden Creek where it was joined with the upper Flat River. Valley glaciers arrived from the southwest and cut their way through the land, dividing the South Nahanni River from Flood and Jorgenson Creeks. After the glaciers departed, the waters of the upper South Nahanni and Flat Rivers and Diamond Creek flowed through these "breached divides" and carved the drainages which you see today. This doubled the size of the South Nahanni River's catchment basin, resulting in the dramatic scale of the canyon system and falls. In summary, the present flow of this section of the river is considered discordant with the overall geological structure of the land as caused by glaciation.

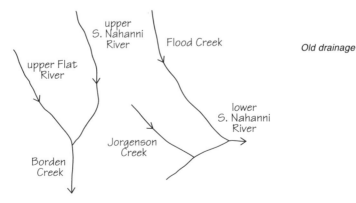

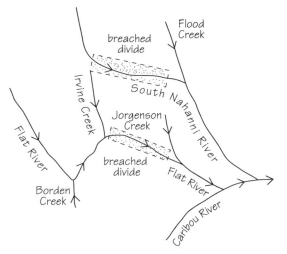

Today's drainage

• Towards Moose Ponds the tightly folded sedimentary rock is oriented along a northwest to southeast axis, thereby providing a valley for the headwaters of the South Nahanni River. This orientation has also provided a home for Broken Skull River, Irvine Creek, Hell Roaring Creek, Flood Creek, and Clearwater Creek. East of Clearwater Creek, however, the bedrock folds change to a north-south orientation which reflects the flow of Wrigley and Vera Creeks.

• First, Second and Third Canyons offer examples of a discordant relationship between geologic structure and drainage [35, 36, 37]. These canyons are called "antecedent" since the meandering course of the river was established on a flat plain before the mountain-building process took effect. As a result, the original meandering course continued to entrench itself as the mountains lifted around it. This is also true of the Meilleur River and Prairie Creek which essentially flow against the grain of the surrounding geological structure.

Fluvial Landforms

V-Form Valleys

V-form valleys are the most common fluvial landform outside of pre-glaciated areas in Nahanni. As the name suggests, the valley walls are v-shaped and the valley floor is only a little wider than the stream itself. This is considered an immature feature associated with easily eroded rocks and a small volume of water. In Nahanni, V-form valleys are mostly found west of Third Canyon in those areas not recently glaciated.

Consequent Canyons

Consequent canyons are created by topographical gradient and fluvial erosion. In Nahanni, they are well developed and occur on steep mountain sides and plateaus. The largest, located just north of Nahanni Plateau, is 30 kilometres long and over 1,000 metres deep. Lafferty Canyon [34] is another good example.

Antecedent Features

These features are considered "antecedent" because their formation pre-dates the formation of the surrounding mountains and plateaus. Nahanni's antecedent canyons, rivers and streams, such as the Meilleur River, Prairie Creek, Clearwater Creek and First, Second, and Third Canyons are unique. In fact, they are the only examples of this type in Canada and are extremely rare world wide.

When was the last time you paddled in the mountains down a relatively fast, *meandering* river? Seems a little strange doesn't it? As you know, mountain rivers normally flow relatively straight and fast with only minor bends and twists. So why is the southern portion of the South Nahanni so different? The answer lies in the formation of the canyons.

Antecedent canyons are created by a distinct series of events. First, a river is born on flat terrain and, therefore, assumes a meandering coarse. Then, mountains begin to rise while the river continues to erode and entrench itself. Since the land rises at a slower rate than the river entrenchment, the river is able to maintain its original meandering course even though its speed has increased. The slow rate of land uplift is the key factor in this process. For example, it has been estimated that the uplift of Nahanni Plateau, where First Canyon is located, was approximately 0.5 to 1.0 millimetres every 1,000 years. The perfect balance of uplift, river erosive power, rock resistance and rock structure are required for antecedent canyon formation, hence its rarity.

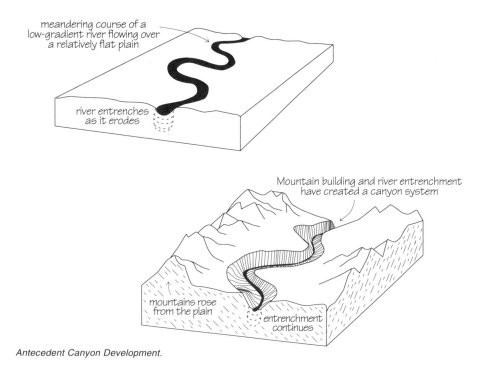

Antecedent Canyon Development.

To some people the numbering of the canyons seems backwards; however, they reflect the sequence in which they were discovered. Actually, we're the ones going backwards!

Third Canyon [35] When the South Nahanni cut into the weaker shales and thin limestone of the Funeral Range, this material eroded at a greater rate, which is why the walls of Third Canyon are lower than those of the other two. The canyon is 35 kilometres long and has a river gradient of 1.5 m/km. During high water, a riffle forms in The Gate. Otherwise there are no rapids. To the east of, or behind The Gate lies the most recent cut-off meander in the canyon system [38]. The Gate was formed when the river found a soft pocket of rock in the canyon wall and cut away at it until the cave broke through to the other side. The roof of the cave has since collapsed. Pulpit Rock [39] is the remnants of one of the old cave walls.

Second Canyon [36] is 14 kilometres long and separated from Third Canyon by a short stretch of river. Here the river pierces the Headless Range with a gradient of 1.3 m/km. There are no rapids. The downstream section boasts the largest meander along the modern river called the Great Spur [45].

First Canyon [37] The river in First Canyon cuts through the southern end of the Nahanni Plateau anticline. The canyon is 26 kilometres long and has two very old cut-off meanders or oxbows [46] which originally extended its length to 40 kilometres. The river falls 33.5 metres or 1.3 m/km. George's Riffle and Lafferty's Riffle are the only rapids and are the result of fluvial deposits of rock on the river bottom from upstream tributaries. At their highest, the canyon walls tower 900 metres above the river and are the highest canyon walls in the park, possibly in all of Canada.

While canyon features are normally associated with very young rivers with rapids and fast treacherous sections, this is not, as we have seen, true of the South Nahanni's 75-kilometre frolic through the canyons. That's why you will sometimes hear the river called "the fraudulent river." The cut-off meanders or oxbows have decreased its length through these canyons by 25 percent, while the river has entrenched itself about 1,500 metres below the land on which it was born. It's interesting to think that had the area been glaciated, these canyons would likely not be here today.

Virginia Falls and Fourth Canyon [40]

Virginia Falls is one of the wonders of North America. To witness its immense power is a truly humbling experience. In order to appreciate these magnificent falls, visitors should understand how Fourth Canyon was actually carved twice by two different waterfalls.

Before the Wisconsinan glacial period, the South Nahanni was located one or two kilometres south of its present position, about where Marengo Creek lies today. During this period the site near the present falls location was occupied by a spur or shoulder of Sunblood Mountain.

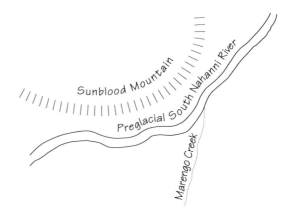

During the advance of the valley glaciers this spur was removed and replaced by a ramp sloping to the southeast.

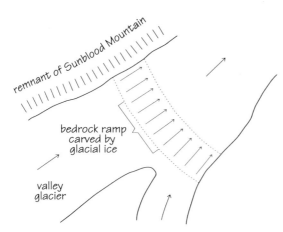

Till deposited by glaciers blocked the preglacial river course and diverted the river to the north where it found the newly carved valley and ramp. Here, the river carved a falls which eroded and left a gorge behind.

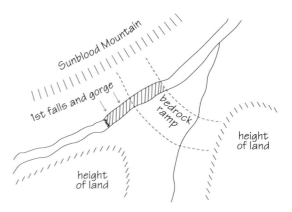

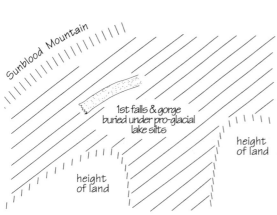

During a subsequent glaciation, Glacial Lake Nahanni completely filled the gorge and covered the falls with silts and clays.

After the lake drained, the river found its way back to the previous gorge, but this time further downstream, past the location of the old falls. This old falls remains buried by debris, roughly under the present location of the portage trail or slightly to the west. Under its new course, the river cleaned out the old lake sediments from the gorge and carved a new extension.

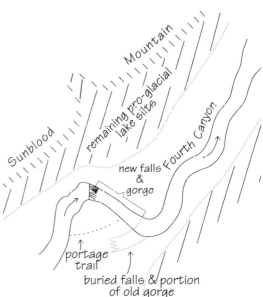

So, as you can see, Fourth Canyon developed very differently from the other canyons. It was not carved by the entrenchment of the river, but instead by the erosional force of the ancient and contemporary Virginia Falls. So, Fourth Canyon is really not a true canyon; perhaps a better name for it would be Virginia Gorge.

Today, Virginia Falls actually consists of two falls separated by a central stack unofficially named Mason Rock. The upper fall is 89.9 metres high and the lower fall 52 metres. When viewed from below, the four acres of whitewater that comprise the falls are truly awe-inspiring. The entire drop, including Sluice Box rapids [41], is close to 117 metres, twice the height of Niagara Falls. The approximate rate of canyon growth since the passing of the second Glacial Lake Nahanni is estimated at 4 millimetres/year.

Rotational Slumps

Slumps occur when water creates a slippery layer under a block of soil. Eventually the mass becomes so unstable that all it needs to slide is a trigger. This trigger is provided by a river or stream that cuts the front or "footing" from the block, thereby removing its support. On one occasion, at the foot of Sunblood Mountain, I observed a slump which had just slid on a layer of permafrost.

There are over 87 large, recent, or well-preserved rotational slumps in the park. The most obvious occur along the river, close to the exit from Second Canyon into Deadmen Valley [44*]. It was here, in 1986, that a slump threatened to nearly dam the river. Trees perched on a slump point and pointing in all directions are referred to as "drunken forests."

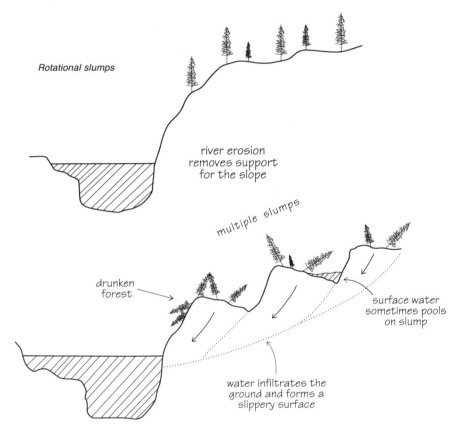

Rotational slumps

river erosion
removes support
for the slope

multiple slumps

drunken
forest

surface water
sometimes pools
on slump

water infiltrates the
ground and forms a
slippery surface

*Top right: A peak in the Nahanni Range.
Interesting bluffs and canyons have been created
as a result of drainage down the steep mountain side.*

*Bottom right: Third Canyon, showing river
meanders and a high water channel.
During high water, an island is formed.*

Alluvial Fans and River Deltas

Prairie Creek Fan [42] was born and grew as the fast-moving creek slowed down as it neared the South Nahanni and deposited its load. Over time this process has continued and now the fan is the largest of over a hundred alluvial fans located in the park, occupying 15 square-kilometres. In Deadmen Valley its front edge forms a four-kilometre arc which continues to push the South Nahanni River into the far bank.

Glacial Lake Tetcela left about 430 metres of silt and clay at the mouth of Prairie Canyon, plugging the original stream mouth. For some reason, instead of resuming its previous course and eroding this silt plug away, Prairie Creek found a weakness in the bedrock and carved its way through the rock to the South Nahanni. The trail leading into the canyon traverses this silt plug [43].

Although The Splits [13*] was formed in a similar manner to an alluvial fan, it is actually considered a river delta. If you are fortunate enough to travel the South Nahanni several times, you will undoubtedly notice how quickly The Splits can change, always presenting a navigational challenge.

The following fluvial landforms are considered:

Rare/unique in the world

- [38] a cut-off meander in an antecedent canyon (The Gate).
- [45] the Great Spur, a regular, in-growing river entrenchment 1320 metres deep (Second Canyon).
- [46] a cut-off meander with regular asymmetry due to steady growth. It is now a separate 425 metre-high mountain (First Canyon).

Rare/unique in Canada

- [35, 36, 37] Third, Second and First Canyons. The largest true river canyons in Canada.
- [40] Virginia Falls and gorge.
- [47] bedrock terracing with in-growing and in-trenching canyon development (Third Canyon). No other known occurrence in Canada.
- [48] dolomite badlands, extensive ravines cut into the walls of Prairie Creek Canyon.
- [43] silt plug, one of the two mouths of Prairie Creek.
- [34] an excellent example of a consequent canyon (Lafferty Canyon).

The best examples of more common park features

- [49] Rabbitkettle and Jackfish Rivers. The best examples of unconstrained river-meander channels in the park.
- [13*] unconstrained river braiding (The Splits).

- [50] [42] major alluvial fans at the mouths of Flood Creek and Prairie Creek.
- [51] multiple river terraces cut into silts and delta deposits. These occur at the mouths of Irvine Creek and the Caribou River in the Flat River valley, and east of Yohin Ridge along the South Nahanni River.
- [44*] large-scale, multi-rotational slumps in Deadmen Valley.

Aolian Features

The Sand Blowouts [14] located on the southeast slopes of Mattson Mountain are the only feature of this type in the park and are quite rare at this latitude. Wind is the chief erosional force as it erodes the soft sandstone into arches, pinnacles and smooth, rounded sculptures similar to the work of sculptor Henry Moore.

Terms useful in describing Nahanni's landforms

Till is unsorted rock debris that has been deposited by advancing or melting glaciers. These deposits are found mainly at the northwest and southeast ends of the park.

Glaciofluvial materials are sands and gravels deposited by glacial meltwater. These deposits are found in patches on Yohin Ridge and at the confluence of the Rabbitkettle and Nahanni Rivers.

Lacustrine deposits are primarily comprised of silts and clays left on the beds of proglacial lakes (lakes formed immediately in front of a glacier). They are found up the trunk valleys of the Flat River and possibly in the Rabbitkettle area.

Aeolian deposits result from wind action. The Sand Blowouts can be seen only after a major swamp bushwhack followed by a climb up the slopes of Mattson Mountain [14].

Nival areas have snow cover which lasts throughout the year.

Fluvial deposits are those left by moving water and consist of bars, deltas, fans, and dry-channel floors of boulders, sorted gravel, sand, and floodplain material. These are found in narrow strips along the sides and confluences of trunk rivers and streams. The Splits [13*] are a good example of a fluvial landform.

Colluvial material is the unsorted rock and finer debris that has collected as a result of the material moving down a slope.

Organic deposits are associated with poorly drained areas and consist of peats and organic mucks found in flat, vegetated flood plains. In Nahanni they often cover silt deposits which keep the organics from draining. On the tour to Rabbitkettle Hotsprings you walk through an organic deposit just before arriving at the Rabbitkettle River. This, by the way, is a great spot to find orchids and bears!

Nahanni's Alpine and Continental Glacial History

Basically, there are three types of glaciers generally differentiated by their size. Continental glaciers are the largest, consisting of massive ice sheets that at one time covered most of North America. The second and smallest are called mountain, valley or alpine glaciers and they are the type that has influenced and to a certain extent still influences the Nahanni area. Piedmont glaciers, the third type, are formed by the joining of several alpine glaciers.

Continental Glaciation

Nahanni escaped the full force of the last glacial advance, the Wisconsinan, which ended about 10,000 to 12,000 years ago. There are two possible reasons for this. First, the larger St. Elias and Logan mountain ranges may have blocked the majority of moist westerly air from reaching the Nahanni region, thereby creating a rain-shadow effect. Second, surrounding large ice sheets may have drawn moist air away from the Nahanni, thereby preventing the creation or spread of large glaciers.

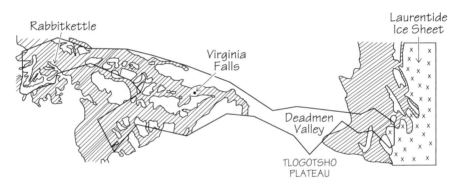

Possible maximum extent of glaciation in Nahanni within the last 130,000 years.

Although the Laurentide Ice Sheet only reached as far as the eastern edge of the Nahanni Range, its influence on the entire region has still been quite significant.

Here are four example of Continental Glaciations:

• Between Mattson and Twisted Mountains there is a two-kilometre breach where the sandstone was carved out by a finger of the Laurentide. This ice sheet left its mark on the southeast corner of Mattson Mountain where you can see the park's best example of lateral scouring [15*]. Other evidence includes a large lateral moraine, three kilometres long by 100 metres wide, on Mattson's north slope. If you're careful, you may spot a rock glacier two kilometres south of this moraine and on the same slope [16].

• Kame and kettle topography can be found on the west side of Yohin Ridge [32]. This feature consists of a series of small ponds separated by ridges of rock debris up to 40 metres high, deposited by the melting of stagnant glacial ice. Since this feature is so worn, it was likely created before the Wisconsinan glaciation.

• Glacial erratics are located on the east flank of Nahanni Plateau but are more easily seen along Lafferty Creek [17]. They consist of greenstone and other igneous rocks which were carried by the ice from the Canadian Shield, located about 250 kilometres to the east. Their weathered condition suggests that they were also deposited by a pre-Wisconsinan glaciation. Some of the finer till accompanying the erratics was washed into caves on the north side of First Canyon including Grotte Valerie where 350,000-year-old stalactites have been found growing on the till. So it follows that the glaciation which deposited the till and erratics known as the "First Canyon Glaciation," must have occurred over 350,000 years ago. This suggests that most of Nahanni's features are at least this old.

• Finally, the creation of extensive glacial lakes has had a very significant impact on the area.

Alpine Glaciation

In the alpine regions, glaciation during the Wisconsinan extended east no further than the Rabbitkettle area. In the valleys, however, one pre-Wisconsinan glacier may have reached as far as Third Canyon and at least two other valley glaciers made it to the area now occupied by Virginia Falls. Today, alpine glaciation is restricted to the higher elevations of the Ragged Range.

Nahanni's Alpine Glacial Features In Nahanni, the Hole-in-the-Wall area [18] exhibits the best examples of relatively new alpine glacial features including cirques and horned peaks. This area is also called the Nahanni Needles; named after granite pillars which are excellent for technical rock climbing.

Above Virginia Falls you can see several examples of U-shaped valleys cut from the bedrock by valley glaciers. Perhaps the best way to appreciate this is to climb to the summit of Sunblood Mountain. From here, you can see the broad U-shaped valley of the South Nahanni to the northwest, its shape contrasting sharply with the area downstream from the falls where little or no glaciation has left the canyon system untouched. Actually, since Third Canyon is so straight for the first two kilometres, some people believe a valley glacier of pre-Wisconsinan vintage had entered the canyon previously.

The depth of these valley glaciers is revealed by trim lines left on mountain sides. Trim lines result from the contrast between frost-shattered rocks that lay above the glacier surface during glaciation and the smooth glacier-worn rock below. While in the Rabbitkettle area you can easily distinguish a series of trim lines on the east side of the South Nahanni [19*]. In this area, the valley glacier is estimated to have been six kilometres wide and 500 metres deep.

Not all alpine glacial features are located in the northwestern half of the park. For example, at the abandoned meander in First Canyon the river carved out a bowl in the north face of the canyon wall which at one time supported a small cirque glacier [20]. This is a unique site — the first recorded instance of an abandoned river meander supporting a glacier.

Glacial Lakes

Glacial Lake Nahanni and Tetcela Proglacial lake deposits are those left by the glacial lakes which formed when a continental glacier dammed the river and stopped it from flowing between Twisted and Mattson Mountains. The water continued to back up until it found spillways down side valleys. Two primary spillways flowed down Mary River and May Creek [21]. Several terraces above the South Nahanni suggest the glacial lake did not drain in a single catastrophic event but rather in stages.

In total, three glacial lakes occurred in concert with the South Nahanni River, all three likely lasting for 10,000 years or more. The smallest, Glacial Lake Tetcela, rose 200 metres above the current river level in First Canyon and extended to the head of Third Canyon. Glacial Lake Nahanni formed on two different occasions, completely covering the old location of Virginia Falls where about 40 metres of silt was deposited. The second Glacial Lake Nahanni filled First Canyon to about 360 metres above the current river level and extended up the valley as far as Rabbitkettle River.

The deposits left by these lakes consist of sand, silt and clay. While on the river you'll hear the silt singing as it scrapes the bottom of your boat. This silty song suggests the river has not yet eroded the proglacial lake deposits from the river bottom. Can you imagine the tumultuous ride through the canyons that would result if the silt wasn't there to smooth the way over the rocky riverbed?

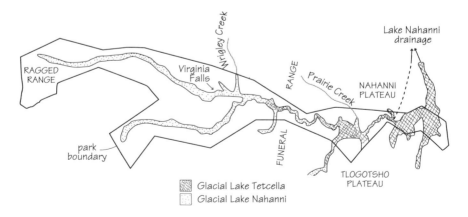

Figure 14: The maximum estimated extent of Glacial Lake Tetcela and both occurrences of Glacial Lake Nahanni.

Photo: Doug Eastcott

The icefield at the head of Brintnell Creek

In Canada, and in much of North America, a landscape that has not been drastically altered by glaciation is relatively rare. In this respect Nahanni is truly unique. Its landscape has been left virtually unaltered and exposed to other erosional processes. This is the primary reason for its wide variety of landforms.

The following glacial features are considered:

Rare/unique in the world

- [22*] interlinking glacial scour-troughs and solifluction sheets incised by glacial marginal channels (Hole-in-the-Wall Valley).
- [20] a cut-off antecedent river meander at one time occupied by a cirque glacier (First Canyon).

Rare/unique in Canada

- [23] ice-moulded bedrock with a network of meltwater channels (downstream of Flood Creek).

- [24*] highly weathered glacial till including erratics from the Canadian Shield (Nahanni Plateau and Lafferty Creek).

The best examples of more common park features:

- [25] a horned peak (Hole-in-the-Wall).
- [26] a U-shaped alpine glacial valley (Rabbitkettle Valley).
- [27] solifluction features (widespread).
- [28*] a glacial marginal meltwater-channel cut in bedrock containing small karst sinkholes (near Hell Roaring Creek).
- [29] a glacier-breached divide (widespread throughout area)
- [30*] proglacial lake floors: a) of second Glacial Lake Nahanni (Caribou River), b) of Glacial Lake Tetcela (Clausen Creek, Deadman Valley).
- [31*] intensively dissected first and second Glacial Lake Nahanni deposits (Flat River confluence).
- [32] kame and kettle features (north end of Yohin Ridge on river left).
- [33] a terminal moraine of the Laurentide Ice Sheet (Mattson Mountain).

Terms useful in describing Nahanni's glacial and periglacial features

Periglacial features are those that have developed in a cold climate where frost-related processes dominate. Frost-shattered rock is an example.

Solifluction ground includes features created when frozen soils have melted and flowed down a slope.

A **moraine ridge** consists of unsorted material deposited at the sides and/or terminal end of a glacier.

A **cirque** is an alpine feature caused by erosion from a cirque glacier. It resembles what you might expect if a giant - sized ice cream scoop removed a piece of mountain side.

A **rock glacier** has all the characteristics of an ice glacier except the ice is buried under a mantle of rock.

A **breached divide** is a height of land removed by glaciation.

Horn peaks are mountain peaks eroded by alpine cirque glaciers into horn-like shapes.

Glacial spillways are drainage channels cut by the outflow of proglacial lakes.

Glacial erratics are large and small rocks picked up, carried, and deposited by a glacier in an area far from their origin.

Kame and kettle topography consists of a series of potholes separated by small ridges of unsorted glacial debris. These are caused by deposition from a stagnant glacier.

Nahanni's Permafrost and Periglacial Landforms

An area is considered to be permafrost when the ground remains frozen continuously for two or more years. Nahanni is located in an area having widespread permafrost except in warmer soils such as on southwest-facing mountain slopes or near bodies of water.

Periglacial landforms, created by the effects of freeze-thaw action on soil and rock, are very active in this area of the Territories. During the last glacial period, much of the Nahanni region was free of the insulating properties of snow and ice and consistently exposed to very cold atmospheric temperatures. This provided perfect conditions for the creation of extensive periglacial landforms. Today the climate is much warmer, and now relatively minor periglacial processes strive to maintain these extensive features.

Frost Polygons

The frost-sorting of material into frost polygons or stone polygons occurs on relatively flat ground. One explanation for their formation suggests that debris is vertically lifted from the surface as it expands during freezing, and then as the ground melts the material cannot resume its original position since the original space has been filled with finer debris falling into the holes created. Therefore, the coarse material migrates across the surface. These polygons usually occur together in a series and can be recognized by their raised rims of coarser material which progressively grades to finer material in the centre. The reason for the polygon shape remains a mystery. Frost polygons can be seen on the south mound of Rabbitkettle Hotsprings [52*]. It is strange that this should occur so close to the mound's vent, since the proximity of the warm water should have prevented the polygons from forming. A better example, although less accessible, can be seen on Tlogotsho Plateau [52*].

Frost Stripes

Frost stripes, or stone stripes, develop in a manner similar to frost polygons, but since they develop on steeper slopes they form an alternating pattern of larger and smaller stone stripes oriented downhill. Examples are hard to find, but in the park they are most common on the Nahanni Plateau north of First Canyon. A better example can reportedly be found on the east-facing slope descending to the cut-off meander at The Gate [53*].

Frost Shattered Rock

Frost-shattering is the most significant periglacial process in effect today. Rocks are shattered when tons of pressure is exerted by water entering a rock and expanding by nine percent its original volume as it freezes. These tremendous pressures simply tear the rock apart. There are additional factors to consider, such as the directional growth of ice crystals which can accentuate the pressure applied to the rock.

Patterned ground on Tlogotsho Plateau.

Rock Glaciers

Rock glaciers look and behave much like regular alpine glaciers, except that their surface is totally covered by a mantle of rock debris, making them hard to distinguish from other talus slopes. There are few good examples in the Nahanni area, although a large one, two kilometres long and 600 metres wide, is located near Irvine Valley. A more easily viewed rock glacier lies on the north slope of Mattson Mountain near The Splits [16]. This one is 1,600 metres long and 950 metres wide.

Solifluction Lobes

Solifluction lobes [27] occur throughout the park in various sizes. Forty seven very large solifluction lobes (up to five kilometres long and hundreds of metres wide), have developed mainly where outcrops of weak shales sit on slopes angled at 10 to 40 degrees. They form when the active layer or top layer of permafrost melts and saturates the ground which becomes heavy and slides downhill. Large lobes are the result of several thousands of years of periglacial action. As new surfaces are exposed to surface heating they slide, thereby continually feeding the lobe. These features, widespread throughout the region, are easy to spot from the air but are not so easily seen from the ground.

Thaw Ponds

Thaw ponds [54*] are created when permafrost melts, leaving a depression that eventually fills with rain and snow meltwater. They are also called "thermokarst features" because of their resemblance to karst sinkholes. This process is still very active in the Nahanni area with several examples throughout the region. For instance, you can see hundreds of thaw ponds as you fly over the MacKenzie Plains on your way into Nahanni. Other examples lie between Virginia Falls and Flood Creek By the way, these are great areas to spot moose and other wildlife.

The following permafrost and periglacial features are considered the best examples in the park:

- [16] rock glacier (Mattson Mountain)
- [27] solifluction sheets (widespread)
- [54*] thaw ponds (Mackenzie Plains, along South Nahanni Valley between Virginia Falls and Rabbitkettle)
- [53*] stone frost stripes (The Gate)
- [52*] frost polygons (south mound of Rabbitkettle Hotsprings, Tlogotsho Plateau)

Nahanni's Karst and Pseudokarst Landforms

Karst landforms are created by the chemical dissolving of limestone. This is not a process involving physical erosion. Briefly, the calcite portion of limestone is dissolved by water containing a weak carbonic acid, such as is found in rain water. The carbon dioxide in soil also combines with rainwater to strengthen this acid. The amount of carbon dioxide in soil is very high in areas with lush vegetation cover, so tropical areas are more likely to have well-developed karst features. Although the rate of karstification is not known for Nahanni, general rates may vary from 2 to 140 m^3/km^2/year.

As mentioned above, karst features are most commonly associated with humid tropical climates, but because Nahanni escaped the last glacial advance its features have had lots of time to develop. As a result, Nahanni karst is not only a rare development at this latitude but also one of the best examples of karst landscape in the world.

Although karst features do not form in dolomite, this rock does play an important role in maintaining the dynamic underground drainage associated with Nahanni's karst. The large volume of water pouring from Whitespray Spring in First Canyon is an example of this [55].

Karst Features

Karst landforms can be divided into surface features and underground features such as cave systems. A few of the many surface karst landforms are:

- *Karren* which are small solution pits, runnels, and grooves in bedrock. Individually, these are relatively small (up to 10 metres long), but collectively they can cover a large area, in which case they form a feature called *limestone pavement*.

- *Dolines* are round, funnel or bowl-shaped sinkholes ranging in size from 10 to 1000 metres in diameter. Rock towers and arches also form in association with dolines.

- *Poljes* are similar to dolines except they are generally much larger and have a clay bottom which inhibits the karstification process. They enlarge as the surrounding limestone walls dissolve. Sometimes the bottoms are filled with water (see photo on pages 136-137).

- *Dry valleys* and *dry gorges* are long (over 1,000 metres) linear features formed by streams that dissolved the rock and then drained, the water being diverted into caves or dolines.

- *Karst streets* are long, linear canyon-like features created when the land separating a series of aligned dolines and/or poljes dissolved.

In Nahanni, all these features are present north of First Canyon on the Nahanni Plateau [56*]. Here, you'll find limestone pavement, hundreds of sinkholes, rock towers up to 50 metres high, about 50 natural bridges, poljes, and eight major dry canyons. One of several karst streets is nine kilometres long, while not too far away a number of karst streets have interconnected to form a complex labyrinth.

Subsurface features consist of cave systems, also called solution passages which are created as water dissolves its way through bedrock. Of over 200 cave entrances in the Nahanni area, 120 are located along the walls of First Canyon. Most are plugged with ice or silt near their entrances but three, including Grotte Mickey and Grotte Valerie, have been explored for more than a thousand metres.

Grotte Valerie [57] is the most famous of the Nahanni caves. In total, there are two kilometres of passages reached via three entrances. These tunnels formed as water drained downward from sinkholes on the plateau, creating four separate passages — Stalactite Gallery, Ice Lake, Dead Sheep Passage, and the Crystal Passage — which over time, became linked into a single large system. For a more detailed description of Grotte Valerie with photographs see page 89.

Opposite top: A general view of the karstlands. In the foreground are some examples of Dolines and Solution Streets.
Opposite bottom: Aerial view of karstlands showing sinkholes and other karst features.

photo: Doug Eastcott

The karstlands. A double arch in the cliffs above Raven Lake.

Pseudokarst Features

Throughout the world psuedokarst (false karst) features are relatively rare and usually poorly developed, except in Nahanni, that is, where they are abundant and well developed. Superficially, they resemble a true karst feature but are created in a different manner.

- *Rabbitkettle Hotsprings.* This fantastic landform is both a volcanic feature because of the source of its heated water, and a pseudokarst feature because it involves the dissolving and deposition of calcium carbonate or tufa or travertine. These mounds [58] are the largest of their type in Canada and possibly in any sub-arctic environment in the world. Built on rock deposited during the last glacial advance, the mounds are less than 10,000 years old.

  From a vent located on each of the two mounds, a spring of water flows at temperatures ranging from 20.5°C to 21.5°C. It's amazing to think that while Virginia Falls almost freezes solid during cold winters, these springs keep running. That's because they originate from a very deep water table over 2,000 metres down where the water receives its warmth. As it rises, the water dissolves the limestone bedrock and becomes supersaturated with calcium carbonate. This mineral is then deposited or precipitated as the water reaches the surface, cools, and loses its capacity to maintain the solution. The tufa is deposited as the water flows over the surface of the mound. In some cases the deposits form large rims containing bathtub-sized pools. These are called gours, while smaller versions are called rimstone dams. The mound grows as the stream slowly rotates around the mound from the central vent. Currently, the water seems to be rotating around the mound in a clockwise direction. It probably takes decades for the stream to make one complete rotation.

  The north mound is the largest of the two, with vertical walls 20 metres high and a base-diameter of 70 metres. The vent maintains its large diameter to the depth of the mound.

  The south mound is much less developed for two reasons. First, less water emanates from the vent and, second, the slower rate of deposition leaves the mound vulnerable to frost-shattering and weathering.

- *Piping sinkholes* Basically, piping sinkholes are caused by the mechanical movement of fine material, such as silt, from the bottom and sides of a depression down through a coarse pebble and rock substrate into the water table. From here the material is carried away by connecting "pipes" or underground streams that can be several centimetres in diameter. The process is similar to sand disappearing through a funnel. Over time this erosion produces small lakes and ponds with a very coarse substrate. In Nahanni, the ingredients for these features are readily available — proglacial lake silts overlying coarser glacial till, and the presence of a river to receive the sinkhole drainage.

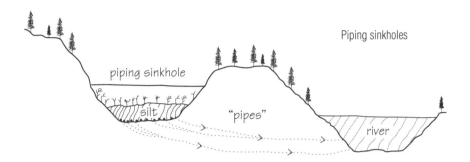

There are 30 piping sinkholes in the Rabbitkettle area and more than 50 surrounding Yohin Lake [59]. In fact, Rabbitkettle Lake likely resulted from the joining of two large piping sinkholes. You can see this from the air as you fly over the lake. These sinkholes are important to several wildlife species, particularly northern pike which re-group each winter at Yohin Lake into a single deep sinkhole while the shallower holes freeze over and become starved of oxygen. Over time, local natives have learned of the pike's winter tricks and now set nets into the ice to catch the fish concentrated in this one sinkhole.

The following karst and pseudokarst features are considered rare and/or unique in the world:

- [58] tufa mounds at Rabbitkettle Hotsprings. They are the only feature of this type and scale in Canada and the only occurrence in the world on permafrost terrain.

- [57] Grotte Valerie. The most significant cave system yet recorded in a sub-arctic environment.

- [56*] Karstlands. An area containing a labyrinth of poljes, towers, natural bridges, dolines, sinkholes, karst streets, and dry valleys. Unique in the world, especially at this latitude.

Earthquakes?

I haven't yet mentioned the impact of earthquakes. People often associate this phenomena with San Francisco and the Pacific coast, but Nahanni also has its fair share. On October 6, 1985, while I diligently shuffled paper in the warden office at Nahanni Butte, an earthquake measuring 6.6 on the Richter scale struck. Books fell off shelves, trees swayed, and gates swung to and fro. For once I was glad I was in the office instead of plying my way through a canyon. There were tremors for the rest of that Fall. During the Fall of 1988, another large earthquake hit the area. Although, to my knowledge, the effects of this particular event have not been documented, several large earth slumps and rock falls occurred throughout the area.

Fur, Feathers, and Fins

Normally, wildlife diversity decreases as latitude increases, but not so for Nahanni where 51 mammal species and over 170 bird species have been observed. There are two reasons for this. First, the Nahanni region of the Territories is populated by wildlife from two zoogeographic stocks, the Holoarctic and Temperate North American. Species from the Holoarctic stock originated in Asia and are thought to have crossed into North America via the Beringia land bridge which spanned Siberia and Alaska during a period of lower sea levels. The Temperate North American stock includes species that migrated north following the retreat of continental glaciers.

The second reason for Nahanni's wildlife diversity is its mountainous topography and variety of landforms which makes available a variety of habitats. This variety is also due to the presence of two boreal forest sections, the Upper Mackenzie and the Alpine-Forest Tundra where arctic-alpine species mingle with southern species that are at their northern-range extensions.

In this part of the Territories, wildlife information is largely restricted to the knowledge of a particular species' presence or absence. Specific information concerning population numbers and trends is largely unavailable.

Mammals

Exotic wildlife species were often introduced by early European settlers to North America, often with catastrophic effects on indigenous flora and fauna. Luckily, Nahanni has escaped such introductions, so the wildlife you encounter along the rivers and in the valleys inhabits the land naturally.

With the exception of the extirpation of wood bison, man has generally had little influence on the faunal character of Nahanni. Although hunting was allowed in the past and continues in the park for First Nations people, such activity has likely had little effect on wildlife populations. Historically, mule and white-tailed deer, coyotes and cougars were unknown, but now their ranges have extended north to Nahanni. In the case of the cougar this is partially due to loss of habitat to human settlement further south.

This isn't to say that all is well, even in this relatively remote part of Canada. We should be concerned for larger predators, such as black and grizzly bears, cougars and wolves, that range outside the protection of our national parks.

Many people still refuse to share territory with these species and often consider such predators a direct threat to human safety, killing them at the first opportunity. Yet we are often the ones who initiate conflicts with predators, as in the case of bears that have come to see us as food providers, often as a result of feeding in our urban landfills. Large predators are also perceived as competitors for game animals such as moose and caribou. Advocates of predator-control programs, mainly hunting guides and outfitters, claim that too many predators, such as wolves, are killing the animals needed to support the hunting industry. In other words, man wishes to become the prime predator for game species, but not for reasons of survival. Unlike other predators, we hunt for sport and trophies to decorate our walls.

The interrelationships between the natural elements of our environment are incredibly complex and varied, and they all play a role in shaping the world around us. In the following section, I provide specific species-related information. However, you mustn't forget all the ingredients such as geology, soils, climate, topography and vegetation that combine to produce the wildlife community in Nahanni.

Dall's Sheep During summer months Dall's sheep head for the alpine tundra like that found on the Tlogotsho and Nahanni Plateaus where they exist on a diet of grasses, sedges and herbs. They can also be seen at mineral licks [60] which provide an important part of the sheep's diet. If taking photographs at salt licks along the river bank, please take care not to disturb the sheep. If continually frightened away, the animals may come to harm, especially the lambs.

Rams live on their own during the summer or travel in bachelor groups, rejoining the ewes and lambs for the fall mating season from mid-November through to mid-December. Lambing occurs roughly during the middle two weeks of the following May. The sheep's main predators include lynx, wolverines, coyotes, wolves and grizzly bears. Small lambs have occasionally met their end in the talons of golden eagles. Those lucky enough to escape predators may live for up to fourteen years before dying of old age.

Mountain Goats Mountain goats rely on high, very steep rock faces for escape and security throughout the year. Therefore, in Nahanni they are predominantly found in the Hole-in-the-Wall and Glacier Lake areas of the Ragged Range. Incredible rock climbers, they are often spotted in the most unimaginable places where they feed on small clumps of grasses, sedges and rushes. They also have keen eyesight and a good sense of smell that helps keep them out of trouble. These animals have been known to live up to twelve years if they can avoid predators such as cougars, grizzly bears, eagles, wolverines and wolves. Unlike Dall's sheep rams, mountain goat billies remain mostly solitary throughout the summer, joining the nannies and kids in the fall. Mountain goats have a matriarchal society with the nannies ruling the roost.

Wood Bison The prehistoric range of this species likely incorporated the area of Fort Simpson and Fort Liard, with a few scattered herds in The Splits area. They disappeared from the region as a result of over-hunting in combination with the severe winters of 1866-1870.

In June 1980, 28 wood bison, transplanted from Elk Island National Park, were released into The Splits area south of the park in an effort to restore the species to its natural range. On occasion, paddlers have spotted the beasts in The Splits, but you are more likely to see only their tracks. They are most often observed around Swan Point on the Liard River. Preliminary indications suggest the population has stabilized at a small number. Little is known of their movements and migrations.

Bison are the largest of Canada's land mammals, with an average adult weight of 420 kg (930 pounds). Only grizzly bears, wolves in packs, and cougars are capable of bringing down a fully-grown adult. Wood bison have good eyesight and an even better sense of smell. They eat mainly grasses, forbs and sedges, and are long-lived, sometimes surviving up to forty years. Mating usually takes place during mid to late summer, with calving occurring from mid-April to June.

Moose Moose are commonly found throughout the year in Nahanni, with an estimated population density of less than 0.5/km^2 for the entire park area.

Moose migrate to higher elevations in the fall and then as winter arrives move back down to lower ground. By doing this they make the best use of food sources and thermal cover. Although they prefer vegetation associated with the early stages of boreal forest development, as is found in recently burned forests, they also enjoy the lowland-meadow and mature coniferous-forest complexes in the river valleys. The area between Rabbitkettle Lake and Virginia Falls is an especially good example. Abandoned river and stream channels also play an important role during the spring and summer months when aquatic vegetation is most abundant. The moose's winter diet consists of willow, red-osier dogwood, balsam fir, aspen, beaked hazel, balsam poplar, and birch twigs. In summer they consume the foliage of these same species, as well as aquatic vegetation, forbs, and grasses. In order to sustain themselves moose need at least five pounds of forage per 100 pounds of body weight per day.

These giants are usually very timid. Cows, however, pose a very real threat when defending their young, and bulls are slightly ornery during the fall rut. Moose can also be quite fierce when munched upon by predators, wolves being chief among this group.

Woodland Caribou The woodland caribou of the Mackenzie Mountains is likely one of the last herds in North America to be left relatively undisturbed. Its territory overlaps that of both the Grant's caribou in the northwest and the barren ground caribou in the northeast (Miller 1982). In Nahanni, caribou are usually found west of The Gate, although some have been seen in Deadmen Valley and as far east as The Splits. Nahanni provides caribou with winter range consisting mainly of subalpine and montane habitat which is dominated by spruce-lichen woodlands and willow-birch-lichen shrub land. More than 400 animals are thought to remain in the area during the winter, although occasional sightings occur during other parts of the year as well.

Special adaptations have made the frigid northern life of the caribou a little easier. Dense fur covers their bodies, including their ears, tail and muzzle, and their large, crescent hooves which, after being worn down by summer travels, grow much larger during the fall and act as snowshoes during winter months. In general, caribou travel in groups and rely on a very acute sense of smell for advance warnings of danger. Their eyesight on the other hand seems very poor. Wolves are the caribou's primary predator and are often seen in association with wintering groups of caribou.

As with most wildlife, caribou are more likely to be spotted while they are feeding, either during the early morning or late evening. Generally, they prefer to bed down during the day.

I have found these critters to be very curious. For example, on one occasion while hiking up Marengo Creek I came upon a lone bull. We were about 20 metres apart when he charged towards me, stopping after half the distance was covered. He bobbed his head around in an apparent attempt to identify what I was (perhaps he thought I was another bull), then he lowered his head, shook his antlers from side to side, and snorted as he pawed the ground. Since I was in a safe spot where I could easily take cover if he became too threatening, I decided to repeat his challenge as best I could. As I shook my head, kicked the ground, and snorted, his head sprang up in surprise and he turned tail and ran back to his original position. Here he must have marshalled himself because he spun around and charged again. After repeating this exchange two more times he finally ran off, never to return. I guess I had a better display. Of course, relishing my new found prowess, I went off in search of his harem!

Mule and White-tailed Deer The southwestern Northwest Territories and southeastern Yukon Territory represent the most northerly extension of the mule deer's range. They seem to have arrived into the Nahanni area during the 1920's when their presence was first recorded by Jack LaFlair in 1929. Since the last sighting of a mule deer was in 1964, it may be that white-tailed deer have now taken over mule deer range.

White-tails, as reported by Mary Kraus, likely arrived in the area in the mid- to late 1960's and have been spotted along the South Nahanni, particularly around the east end of First Canyon and The Splits. With good hearing and eyesight, and an even better sense of smell, white-tails are well equipped for eluding predators such as cougars, lynx, bears and wolves. However, if still caught unaware, they can rely on speeds of up to 60 kilometres per hour to carry them to safety. Fawns are born between May and June and although stubbornly defended by does, are often targeted by predators during this vulnerable period. White-tails have been known to live for up to 10 years in the wild.

Top left: Wolf.
photo: Gillean Daffern

Bottom left: Grizzly crossing South Nahanni.

Top right: Dall's sheep
photo: Gillean Daffern

Bottom right: Cow Moose and young.

171

Elk. Although elk are not found in the Nahanni area according to distribution maps, an experienced outdoorsman once reported a sighting in the Rabbitkettle area. This seems unlikely but who knows?

Wolves Wolves are fairly common in the Park, although their estimated population, between 30 and 75, is a little lower than expected. During my Nahanni travels I was never lucky enough to see a wolf, but I often recall one memorable fall evening when I listened to their haunting calls carried on the night winds over Deadmen Valley. Their tracks are commonly seen on mud and silt bars throughout the region.

Wolves are very smart predators and, while individually capable of attacking and killing prey, they usually hunt in packs in order to more safely and efficiently take large mammals. Their menu includes moose, deer, Dall's sheep, caribou, snowshoe hares, beavers, muskrats, marmots and mice.

Wolves have a very complex social structure which includes a dominant male and female responsible for providing pups for the pack. When individual wolves fight for this honour, it ensures the best genetic stock is carried through the generations. Although the dominant pair are very capable parents, all pack members are responsible for feeding, educating and protecting the pups. Dens have been recorded in the area around the mouths of the Flat River and Prairie Creek and I found what may have been a den just north of the area between the Rabbitkettle warden cabin and the campground. At about two months, pups are carried in their mother's mouths to a new den site, possibly because the old den has become too dirty or flea infested.

Packs are quite loose during the summer, but by early fall pack associations renew. During this period it is common to hear them howl as they become reacquainted.

It's a shame that we are taught through bedtime stories, movies etc. to hate and fear wolves. In many instances this prejudiced understanding of wolves sticks with us for the rest of our lives. Perhaps this is the reason for the disgusting way in which some wildlife management agencies in Canada "manage" wolf populations. Techniques include indiscriminate poisoning, trapping and shooting. By killing off wolves, man increases the populations of game species which are then targeted by "sportsmen's" rifles. A lot of dollars are spent by hunters.

Coyotes and Red Foxes Coyotes have never been seen in the park, although according to distribution maps the Nahanni area is within their range. Red foxes have been spotted within the park only on rare occasions.

Black Bears Black bears are a common sight. Many travellers try to identify them solely by their colour, but this is not a reliable technique as black bears come in several different colours, including variations of black, cinnamon and blonde. It is extremely important that you are able to distinguish between black and grizzly bears because both species behave in different ways and knowledge of these differences is essential to your safety should you have an encounter. You should be familiar with their different tracks as well.

Black bears use many different habitats below treeline and are solitary animals except during the breeding season (mid-June to late July). Usually two to three cubs are born to a litter during January or February while the mother is in hibernation. It remains a mystery how the mother is able to continuously produce milk for her nursing cubs while in this state. The cubs remain with their mother for two years.

Black bears don't see very well, but they have good hearing and rely on a keen sense of smell to find their food. You may see them stand up on their rear legs with their noses held high in the air as they try to identify a scent. Their diet is approximately 75 percent vegetation, with carrion, insects, small mammals and fish making up the rest. In the spring they typically eat sprouting plants and buds high in sugar and protein, switching in summer to fruits such as berries, supplemented by roots and tubers. Black bears generally do not kill larger game such as deer, moose and caribou. On very rare occasions, however, they will attack humans. A rough estimate of the typical home range needed to support one black bear in this region is 220 square-kilometres!

Grizzly Bears Grizzlies are large bears, the males ranging from 250 to 320 kg and the females 200 kg or less. They favour alpine and subalpine environments but can be found all over Nahanni, particularly in the Glacier Lake and Hole-in-the-Wall areas. Their poor eyesight is compensated by excellent hearing and an outstanding sense of smell. Like black bears, they may stand with their noses in the air when trying to identify a scent.

Grizzlies are mostly solitary animals, only associating during the mating season from late June to early July. They become sexually mature at six to seven years of age and, like black bears, hibernating mothers bear two to three cubs during the mid winter. Cubs are about the size of a kitten at birth and grow at an astonishingly rate, reaching 25 kilograms at six months. After a long winter of living in a den from October to May or June, the bears emerge in search of food, the sow watching carefully for wandering boars that would eat her cubs.

Ninety-six percent of their diet consists of green vegetation and berries while the rest is carrion, insects, other mammals and fish. On leaving their dens, grizzlies head for the valley bottoms (i.e. the Rabbitkettle and Virginia Falls areas and the Flat River confluence) where they feed on spring vegetation and on animals that have died over the winter. Spring and summer foods include cow parsnips, angelica, horsetails, the sapwood of deciduous trees, various grasses, hedysarum roots, sedges, Buffaloberry and other berries. One study indicated that hedysarum roots and horsetails represented as much as 60 percent of their total summer diet. It's amazing how grizzlies can attain such a massive size by eating mostly berries, leaves and roots. On page 41 are some ideas to help you from becoming an unwilling percentage of some grizzly's diet!

Lynx Lynx are solitary cats, mostly active during the night when they prowl the boreal forest in search of prey. I once came upon a lynx as it lay contentedly along the river bank. It did not appear afraid. It just lay there and watched me for at least five minutes before casually strolling off into the underbrush. What a beautiful sight!

Excluding their ability to smell, lynx have a range of keen senses. Within their 10 to 12 square-kilometre home ranges they build rough beds under the protection of rocky ledges and fallen trees. In boreal forests, lynx are considered the most important cat predator and are closely linked with snowshoe hare populations. They also eat birds, small rodents, foxes, deer, young sheep and caribou. Other than man, who traps them for fur, wolves and cougars are their primary predators.

Cougars Historically, this region of the Territories was thought to be beyond the range of the cougar. However, there have been recent sightings — three on Prairie Creek Fan and one in the Rabbitkettle area — that suggest Nahanni may be becoming home to more of these cats. Cougars likely extended their northerly range while following white-tailed deer, their menu item of choice. Except for bears, cougars are the largest predators in Canada, with big males reaching lengths of eight feet and weighing up to 270 pounds.

Cougars are solitary and primarily nocturnal. They feed mostly on larger mammals such as deer, moose, sheep and elk, but will also occasionally hunt porcupines, beavers, foxes, lynx and mice. They stalk their prey using much the same technique as a house cat. Once their prey is near, they pounce on its back and sink their powerful jaws into the nape of the animal's neck, breaking it. After making a kill, they drag the carcass off to a secluded place to feed. They like their meat fresh and will not scavenge off old carcasses. If they intend to return to a kill, they will cover the carcass with leaves and other material from the forest floor, thereby masking the scent from nosey scavengers.

Cougars are very shy, so you will be very lucky if you spot one. On the other hand, they have been known to attack and kill humans, especially children, but this is extremely rare; man is more guilty of harming them. In many parts of Canada some hunters consider it sporting to have their dogs chase a cougar up a tree where it can be easily shot. Cougars are beautiful, majestic creatures and deserve our respect and protection even beyond the confines of parks and preserves.

Recommended Field Guides:

Gadd, B **Handbook of the Canadian Rockies**, Corax Press, Jasper 1986.

Whitaker Jr., John **The Audubon Society Field Guide to North American Mammals** Alfred A Knopf 1980.

List and status of mammals in Nahanni

C = common   EX = expected
U = uncommon   ? = uncertain presence
O = occasional   P = present with abundance unknown
R = rare

Note: following the above designations an *e, t,* or v may appear, indicating that this
species' existence is either endangered, threatened, or vulnerable, according to
the Committee on the Status of Endangered Wildlife in Canada (COSEWIC April,
1991).

Species	Status	Comments
Order: _Insectivora_		
Shrew family *(Soricidae)*		
Short-tailed Shrew	C	wide range of low elevation habitats
Dusky Shrew	U	one specimen found near Kraus Hotsprings
Water Shrew	EX	found at Glacier Lake
Arctic Shrew	EX	found at Fort Liard
Pygmy Shrew	EX	
Order: _Chiroptera_		
Smooth-faced bat family (*Vespertillionidae*)		
Little Brown Bat	P	Kraus Hotsprings & Deadmen Valley
Keen's Bat	R	one specimen found at Deadmen Valley & Kraus Hotsprings, a new park record and range extension
Order: _Lagomorpha_		
Pika family *(Ochotonidae)*		
Collared Pika	O	
Hare family *(Leporidae)*		
Snowshoe Hare	C	
Order: _Rodentia_		
Squirrel family *(Sciuridae)*		
Least Chipmunk	C	
Woodchuck	EX	northern limit of range is Fort Simpson / Fort Liard
Species	**Status**	**Comments**

List and status of mammals in Nahanni — continued

Species	Status	Comments
Hoary Marmot	EX	found at Glacier Lake
Arctic Ground Squirrel	C	found in alpine tundra and grassy areas at lower elevations
Red Squirrel	C	
Northern Flying Squirrel	O	may be more common but is very secretive
Beaver family (Castoridae)		
Beaver	C	
Mouse, rat and vole family (Cricetidae)		
Deer Mouse	C	
Bushy-tailed Wood Rat	U	found in the caves of First Canyon
Northern Red-backed Vole	C	
Gapper's Red-backed Vole	EX	northern limit is Fort Liard
Northern Bog Lemming	U	two specimens found on the Flat River
Heather Vole	EX	
Meadow Vole	C	
Tundra Vole	EX	found at high elevations
Long-tailed Vole	C	
Yellow-cheeked Vole	EX	
Muskrat	P	
Jumping mouse family (Zapodidae)		
Meadow Jumping Mouse	R	one found at Kraus Hotsprings
Porcupine family (Erithizontidae)		
Porcupine	P	

Order: *Carnivora*

Species	Status	Comments
Dog, wolf and fox family (Canidae)		
Coyote	EX	within extended range but has never been seen in the area
Wolf	C	
Red Fox	P	

List and status of mammals in Nahanni — continued

Species	Status	Comments
Bear family *(Ursidae)*		
Black Bear	C	
Grizzly Bear	O, *v*	
Weasel and skunk family *(Mustelidae)*		
Marten	C	
Fisher	P	
Ermine	C	
Least Weasel	?	observed by author under Virginia Falls boardwalk
Mink	C	
Wolverine	U, *v*	
Striped Skunk	EX	
River Otter	U	
Cat family *(Felidae)*		
Cougar	?	tracks found near Sunblood Mtn, at Rabbitkettle Lake and on Prairie Creek fan.
Lynx	P	
Order: *Arctiodactyla*		
Deer family *(Cervidae)*		
Woodland Caribou	C	some herds migrate into the park during winter
Mule Deer	?	the last sighting was in 1964
White-tailed Deer	U	
Moose	C	
Bison, goat, muskox and sheep family *(Bovidae)*		
Wood Bison	?, *t*	re-introduced into the park, occasionally seen in The Splits
Mountain Goat	U	seen in the Ragged Range including Hole-in-the-Wall area
Dall's Sheep	C	

Birds

The birds of Nahanni are a mix of Cordilleran, Boreal and Great Plains species. Of the total of 13 orders, 35 families and 170 species recorded in the park area, about 31 percent originate in North America, another 17 percent originate in the "Old World," and nine percent come from South America. The remainder cannot be traced to any specific origin. Only 22 percent of the recorded species for this area remain north for the entire year.

The following is a brief description of some of the threatened or vulnerable bird species:

Trumpeter Swans Seeing a Trumpeter Swan is truly an occasion to remember. This large and majestic white bird is very rare and its preservation is of international importance. Before the European settlement of North America, the swan's breeding range covered an area from Alaska across Canada to Ontario and south to Iowa, Missouri and Indiana in the United States (Mackay 1978). Commercial trade for their skins and feathers and a general loss of habitat has resulted in one of the most dramatic declines of a wildlife species ever recorded. Although their numbers are now on the increase, their limited habitat still places the species in jeopardy. Nahanni provides summer-breeding habitat critical to these birds which over-winter in the tri-state area of Montana, Wyoming and Idaho..

Trumpeter Swans are very territorial and will protect their nests and young to the end. On one occasion while using a helicopter to count swans, nests and eggs, I watched one adult swan defending its nest with such ferocity it appeared willing to wrestle our helicopter to the ground. Other behaviour used for defence and greeting includes the spreading, raising and quivering of wings, head bobbing and trumpeting.

The swans raise one brood per year and lay five to nine eggs in a clutch, usually on an isolated island or on a beaver or muskrat house that is relatively safe from predators (coyotes and Bald Eagles). In seeking proper areas for nesting, Trumpeter Swans also look for a good supply of emergent vegetation, such as reeds and sedges which provide for their rather demanding food requirements of approximately 9 kg/day/adult.

The deep resonant call is reminiscent of a big brass horn and helps to identify the Trumpeter from the Mute and Tundra Swans. An elongated windpipe that forms a high loop in the chest is responsible for this beautiful sound.

Peregrine Falcons The Peregrine Falcon, which derived its name from the Latin for wanderer, is one of the swiftest birds in the world, capable of attaining speeds of up to 290 km/hr. It uses its great speed to overtake other birds. A common hunting strategy is to fly well above its prey, then swiftly dive, colliding in midair with the prey which is usually killed instantly by the extended talons.

By the end of the 1960's the Peregrine Falcon was virtually extinct in the USA and southeastern Canada. Pesticides, especially DDT, resulted in very thin egg shells that could not adequately protect the unborn birds. The banning of DDT in North America in the early 1970's, combined with successful captive breeding programs, has helped to bring the bird back from the brink of extinction. Unfortunately, several Latin American countries are still using DDT and birds overwintering in these countries are still picking up significant quantities of pesticides.

In 1986 I observed a pair of Peregrine Falcons on the canyon wall near the mouth of Lafferty Creek. Unfortunately, despite continued formal surveys by park staff, there have not been any more recent sightings.

Great Gray Owl This owl is the largest of all owls in North America, having a wing span of up to 152 centimetres. It lives in boreal forests where it hunts small mammals such as rabbits, sometimes small song birds and occasionally, fish. Prey is mostly swallowed whole, the owl later regurgitating a pellet containing the bones, fur and feathers. With its very acute sense of hearing, the owl can even hear mice moving under the snow. A soft dive on silent wings (facilitated by the serrated front edge of the first primary feather) allows the bird to approach its prey in silence.

The dish-shaped face enables it to hunt by sound alone. The ability to locate a noise within 1.5 degrees on both the horizontal and vertical plane is a function of the detected time difference a sound reaches each ear and the difference in the intensity of the sound. For example, when a sound is simultaneously heard in each ear at the same intensity, the noise is coming from directly ahead. The owl's ears are connected to specialized cells in the mid brain which interpret the auditory messages.

When lucky enough to discover a Great Gray, I have often found you can approach quite closely before it flies for cover.

Recommended Field Guides:

Peterson Field Guides: Western Birds Houghton Mifflin Co, Boston 1990.

Scotter, George W, & Ulrich Tom J, & Jones, Edgar **Birds of the Canadian Rockies** Western Producer Prairie Books 1990.

Ehrlich, Paul R, Dobkin, David S., Wheye, Darryl **The Birders Handbook** Simon & Schuster Inc. 1988.

National Geographic Society **Field Guide to the Birds of North America** National Geographic Society. Second edition 1987.

Top left: Ruffed Grouse.
Bottom left: Upland Sandpiper.

Top right: Red-tailed Hawk.
Bottom right: Trumpeter Swans.

List and status of birds in Nahanni

Season	S = summer	RES = resident	
	M = migrant	W = winter	
Breeding	B = breeding	NB = not breeding	
	P = possible	EX = expected	
	U = Unknown		
Abundance	C = common	U = uncommon	
	P = possible	R = rare	

Note: following the above designations an *e, t,* or *v* may appear indicating that this species' existence is either endangered, threatened, or vulnerable, respectively, according to the Committee on the Status of Endangered Wildlife in Canada. (COSEWIC April, 1991)

Species	Status		
	Season	Breeding	Abundance
***Order:* Gaviiformes**			
Loon family *(Gaviidae)*			
Common Loon	S	B	C
Yellow-billed Loon	M	NB	R
Arctic Loon	S	B	U
Red-throated Loon	S	B	U
***Order:* Podicipediformes**			
Grebe family *(Podicipedidae)*			
Red-necked Grebe	S	B	C
Horned Grebe	S	B	U
Pied-billed Grebe	S	P	U
***Order:* Anseriformes**			
Swan, goose and duck family *(Anatidae)*			
Trumpeter Swan	S	B	U, *v*
Canada Goose	M	NB	C
White-fronted Goose	M	NB	R
Mallard	S	B	C
Gadwall	S	P	P
Pintail	S	P	U
Green-winged Teal	S	B	C

List and status of birds in Nahanni — continued

	Season	Breeding	Abundance
Blue-winged Teal	S	B	U
American Wigeon	S	P	U
Northern Shoveller	S	P	R
Redhead	S	P	R
Ring-necked Duck	S	P	R
Greater Scaup	M	NB	U
Lesser Scaup	S	B	C
Barrow's Goldeneye	S	B	R
Common Goldeneye	S	B	C
Bufflehead	S	B	C
Old Squaw	M	NB	C
White-winged Scotter	S	P	C
Surf Scotter	S	P	C
Common Merganser	S	P	U
Red-breasted Merganser	S	P	U

Order: Falconiformes

Osprey, kite, eagle, hawk and allies
family (*Accipitridae*)

	Season	Breeding	Abundance
Goshawk	RES	P	U
Sharp-shinned Hawk	S	B	C
Red-tailed Hawk	S	BP	U
Swainson's Hawk	S	BP	R
Golden Eagle	S	BP	U
Bald Eagle	S	B	C
Marsh Hawk	S	B	U
Osprey	S	PB	R

Caracara and falcon family
(*Falconidae*)

	Season	Breeding	Abundance
Gyrfalcon	S	PB	R
Peregrine Falcon	S	PB	R, *t*
Merlin	S	PB	R
American Kestrel	S	B	C

Order: Galliformes

Partridge, grouse, turkey and quail
family (*Phasianidae*)

	Season	Breeding	Abundance
Blue Grouse	RES	B	C

List and status of birds in Nahanni — continued

	Season	Breeding	Abundance
Spruce Grouse	RES	B	C
Ruffed Grouse	RES	B	C
Willow Ptarmigan	WM	UB	U
Rock Ptarmigan	WM	NB	U
White-tailed Ptarmigan	RES	PB	U
Sharp-tailed Grouse	RES	PB	R

Order: Gruiformes

Crane family *(Gruidae)*

Sandhill Crane	M	NB	R

Rail, gallinule and coot family *(Rallidae)*

Sora	S	B	U
American Coot	S	PB	U

Order: Charadriiformes

Plover family *(Charadriidae)*

Semipalmated Plover	M	NB	C
Killdeer	M	NB	R
American Golden Plover	S	OB	R

Sandpipers, phalaropes and allies family *(Scolopocidae)*

Common Snipe	S	B	C
Upland Sandpiper	S	B	U
Spotted Sandpiper	S	B	C
Solitary Sandpiper	S	PB	C
Western Sandpiper	M	NB	R
Greater Yellowlegs	S	PB	U
Lesser Yellowlegs	S	B	C
Pectoral Sandpiper	M	NB	U
Baird's Sandpiper	M	NB	R
Least Sandpiper	S	NB	R
Stilt Sandpiper	N	NB	P
Semipalmated Sandpiper	M	NB	R
Western Sandpiper	M	NB	R
Sanderling	M	NB	P
Northern Phalarope	S	PB	C

List and Status of birds in Nahanni — continued

	Season	Breeding	Abundance
Skua, gull, tern and skimmer family *(Laridae)*			
Herring Gull	S	PB	C
Mew Gull	S	PB	C
Bonaparte's Gull	S	PB	C
Arctic Tern	S	B	C
Black Tern	S	PB	R
Order: Strigiformes			
Typical owl family *(Strigida)*			
Great Grey Owl	RES	PB	U, v
Hawk Owl	RES	PB	R
Great Horned Owl	RES	PB	R
Barred Owl	RES	PB	R
Order: Caprimulgiformes			
Goatsucker family *(Caprimulgidae)*			
Common Nighthawk	S	B	C
Order: Apodiformes			
Hummingbird family *(Trochilidae)*			
Ruby-throated Hummingbird	S	NB	P
Swift family *(Apodidae)*			
Black Swift	S	NB	P
Order: Coraciiformes			
Kingfisher family *(Alcedinidae)*			
Belted Kingfisher	S	PB	C
Order: Piciformes			
Woodpeckers family *(Picidae)*			
Common Flicker	S	B	C
Pileated Woodpecker	S	PB	R
Yellow-bellied Sapsucker	S	B	C
Hairy Woodpecker	RES	B	U
Downy Woodpecker	RES	PB	U

List and Status of Birds in Nahanni — continued

	Season	Breeding	Abundance
Black-backed, Three-toed Woodpecker	RES	B	C
Northern Three-toed Woodpecker	RES	B	C

Order: Passeriformes

Tyrant flycatcher family *(Tyrannidae)*

Eastern Kingbird	S	PB	U
Eastern Phoebe	S	PB	U
Say's Phoebe	S	PB	U
Yellow-bellied Flycatcher	S	PB	R
Alder Flycatcher	S	PB	R
Least Flycatcher	S	PB	U
Western Wood Pewee	S	PB	U
Olive-sided Flycatcher	S	PB	U

Lark family *(Alaudidae)*

Horned Lark	S	PB	C

Swallow family *(Hirundinidae)*

Violet-green Swallow	S	B	C
Tree Swallow	S	B	C
Bank Swallow	S	B	C
Cliff Swallow	S	B	C

Jay, magpies and crows *(Corvidae)*

Gray Jay	RES	PB	C
Common Raven	RES	B	C
Clark's Nutcracker	RES	PB	R

Titmouse family *(Paridae)*

Black-capped Chickadee	RES	PB	C
Boreal Chickadee	RES	B	C

Nuthatch family *(Sitiidae)*

Red-breasted Nuthatch	S	PB	R

Dippers family *(Cinclidae)*

Swainson	RES	PB	R

List and Status of Birds in Nahanni — continued

	Season	Breeding	Abundance
Old World warblers, kinglets, gnatcatchers, Old World flycatchers, thrushes, babblers and allies family *(Muscicapidae)*			
American Robin	S	B	C
Hermit Thrush	S	B	C
Swainson's Thrush	S	B	C
Grey-cheeked Thrush	S	B	U
Mountain Bluebird	S	B	U
Townsend's Solitaire	S	PB	C
Golden-crowned Kinglet	S	PB	R
Ruby-crowned Kinglet	S	PB	U
Black and White Warbler	S	PB	U
Tennessee Warbler	S	B	C
Orange-crowned Warbler	S	PB	U
Yellow Warbler	S	B	C
Magnolia Warbler	S	PB	U
Yellow-rumped Warbler	S	B	C
Black-throated Green Warbler	S	PB	R
Bay-breasted Warbler	S	PB	R
Blackpoll Warbler	S	PB	U
Palm Warbler	S	PB	R
Ovenbird	S	PB	U
Northern Waterthrush	S	PB	U
Mourning Warbler	S	PB	U
Common Yellowthroat	S	PB	U
Wilson's Warbler	S	PB	U
American Redstart	S	PB	R
Wagtail and pipit family (Motacillidae)			
Water Pipit	S	B	C
Waxwing family *(Bombycillidae)*			
Bohemian Waxwing	S	B	C
Shrike family *(Laniidae)*			
Northern Shrike	S	PB	R
Starling family *(Sturnidae)*			
Common Starling	S	B	R
Vireo family *(Vireonidae)*			
Red-eyed Vireo	S	B	U
Philadelphia Vireo	S	PB	R
Warbling Vireo	S	B	U

List and Status of Birds in Nahanni — continued

	Season	Breeding	Abundance
Wood warbler, tanager, cardinal, sparrow, bunting, meadowlark, blackbird and orioles family *(Emberizidae)*			
Red-winged Blackbird	S	PB	U
Rusty Blackbird	S	PB	U
Brown-headed Cowbird	S	PB	U
Western Tanager	S	PB	U
Savanah Sparrow	S	B	U
Vesper Sparrow	S	PB	R
Dark-eyed Junco	S	B	C
Tree Sparrow	S	PB	C
Chipping Sparrow	S	PB	C
Clay-coloured Sparrow	S	PB	U
White-crowned Sparrow	S	B	C
Golden-crowned Sparrow	S	B	U
White-throated Sparrow	S	B	C
Fox Sparrow	S	PB	U
Lincoln's Sparrow	S	B	C
Swamp Sparrow	S	B	U
Song Sparrow	S	PB	U
Lapland Longspur	M	NB	C
Finch family *(Fringillidae)*			
Rose-breasted Grosbeak	S	PB	R
Evening Grosbeak	S	PB	R
Purple Finch	S	PB	R
Pine Grosbeak	RES	PR	R
Grey-crowned Rosy Finch	S	RB	U
Hoary Redpoll	WM	NB	C
Common Redpoll	RES	PB	U
Pine Siskin	S	PB	C
White-winged Crossbill	S	B	C

The following birds have also been seen in the area:

Spotted Sandpiper	Long-tailed Jaeger
Varied Thrush	Northern Harrier
Tennesee Warbler	Northern Goshawk
Red-necked Phalarope	American Dipper

Fish

In Nahanni, lakes are free of ice for a relatively short period of time. Most remain colder than 15°C during the summer, with the exception of Rabbitkettle and Yohin Lakes which are shallower. Cold temperatures limit the growth of fish, the availability of their food, thus affecting their reproductive success. Even warm, shallow lakes do not necessarily contain fish, since these lakes are subject to "winter kill", a phenomena which does not involve the freezing of a lake from top to bottom as many people believe (although this does happen for some shallow portions of Yohin Lake). Winter kill occurs when summer aquatic vegetation dies under the ice and uses up oxygen needed by the fish. The ice layer prevents the surface mixing of oxygen.

The presence of fish in this area is directly linked with Nahanni's glacial legacy. Regions not covered by glacial ice provided refuge for many floral and faunal species, including fish, and as a result, there are fish species in Nahanni that were thought to have survived only in the Mississippi-Missouri Refuge located much further to the south. As well, species which were thought present only in the Alaskan and Central Yukon Refuge have also been found in the South Nahanni drainage. At some point in time, Nahanni must have been connected with these other drainages.

The following are some interesting notes on a few of the more popular fish :

Lake Trout Because this fish is usually found in deep and not too turbid waters (which are in short supply in Nahanni), Lake Trout distribution is somewhat restricted. So far they have been found in only one specific location on the South Nahanni River.

Dolly Varden Generally, this is the species most preferred by anglers in the park. Dolly Varden reach sexual maturity in three to six years and spawn in tributary streams during the autumn. This is one of those species thought to exist only in the Mississippi-Missouri Refuge. It remains a mystery how the fish gained access past Virginia Falls into the upper river. It's possible one of the episodes of Glacial Lake Nahanni may be implicated.

Northern Pike In Nahanni, northern pike are found only in Seaplane Lake and Yohin Lake. This latter population is unique since portions of Yohin Lake freeze to the bottom during the winter and the pike must survive by congregating in adjacent sinkholes that are quite deep. During winter months the Dene from Nahanni Butte village fish these sinkholes to supply themselves and their dogs.

Arctic Grayling Arctic Grayling are found throughout the region in rivers, streams and larger lakes. Northern pike is their main predator.

List of fish in Nahanni

- Lake Trout
- Dolly Varden
- Arctic Grayling
- Burbot
- Slimy Sculpin
- Longnose Dace

- Lake Chub
- Longnose Sucker
- Northern Pike
- Lake Whitefish
- Mountain Whitefish
- Round Whitefish

- Lake Whitefish
- Inconnu
- Spoonhead Sculpin
- Trout-perch
- Spottail Shinner

Amphibians and Reptiles

There is very little data available regarding the amphibians and reptiles of Nahanni. The wood frog is one of only two amphibians proven to live here. One species of toad has been found at Yohin Lake and may be either the Canadian Toad *(Bufo hemiophrys)* or the Boreal Toad *(Bufo boreas boreas).* The Boreal Chorus Frog is only suspected of inhabiting the park. No reptiles have yet been recorded.

Insects

There is no official information concerning these critters. Past wildlife research practices have adopted management principles for those species at or near the top of the food chain, the assumption being that if all was well at this trophic level then those species lower on the food chain must be doing well also. For example, the presence of relatively healthy populations of Alder Flycatchers would indicate a healthy population of flying insects. As a result, very little information directly pertaining to insects is available.

I will make one observation, however; this part of the Territories has plenty of mosquitos! How bad are they? Well, that depends on what you're used to. When I worked as a warden in the park we had contests to see how many "mosys" could be killed in a single slap of the hand. For a while the record stood at 22, not counting smudges. Since then, the tradition has continued and the record now stands at 43! The best place to meet these little bloodsuckers is from The Splits to Blackstone Landing. For the most part, the rest of the upstream river has much fewer "mosys." They tend to be abundant in areas where there is still water, such as ponds, where they can lay their eggs.

Recommended Field Guides:

Petersen Field Guides: Insects (America N of Mexico) Houghton Mifflin Co., Boston 1970.

Petersen Field Guides: Fresh Water Fishes Houghton Mifflin Co., Boston 1991.

Flowering Plants

Botanists generally consider the flora of the Mackenzie Mountains both rich and diverse, and Nahanni's flora especially so, its abundance of species far exceeding that of any area of comparable size in the Northwest Territories. Among plants with a vascular system, Nahanni has 219 genera representing 590 species, a number comprising 66 percent of the genera and half of the species found in the entire Northwest Territories. Given Nahanni's northerly location, this abundance and diversity is unique. Generally, northern climates restrict plant growth and diversity decreases as latitude increases. While most of Nahanni's floral species exist in many other areas of North America, Nahanni represents their north-range limit. A number of these species are also circumpolar and can be found in arctic-alpine or subarctic North America, Europe, and northern Asia. Only ten species have been introduced by man.

Several factors contribute to the great diversity and abundance of plant life. Nahanni has several very specialized habitats variously associated with wet calcareous soils, zones of mists generated by waterfalls, and hot and cold mineral springs. For example, in 1974 a new species, Nahanni Aster (*Aster Nahanniensis*), was found near Wildmint Hotsprings and Old Pot Hotsprings. Unglaciated terrain is home to many rare plant species which may provide future researchers with clues to the postglacial distribution of plants and the special adaptations that have taken place over time. Other special habitats have developed along with periglacial features such as permafrost zones. Finally, Nahanni's proximity to the continental divide and the varied habitats associated with mountainous topography have also contributed significantly to the region's floral diversity.

The First Nations People of North America have been using plants for food, medicines and tools for thousands of years. This tradition was adopted to a more limited extent by Europeans during the pioneer years, but with growing industrialization, manufacturing and food-processing techniques along with greater variety and extended shelf life many of the traditional uses of plants have been forgotten or abandoned. In the last few years, however, there has been a revival of sorts and people are once again making use of the common plants that surround us.

Rather than describe all the species in detail, I have compiled lists of common flowering plants, medicinal and edible plants and plants which are rare to the area. Please realize that all this information came from preliminary studies and is not considered definitive. In the case of medicinal plants, my intent is not to give medical advice or prescribe the use of plants for medical purposes, but only to make you aware of the importance of our natural surroundings.

Obviously, these lists are not sufficiently descriptive for comprehensive identification purposes. In other words, if you have a particular interest in Nahanni's flora, take along a plant identification book. Generally, any book applicable to the Rocky Mountains should help you.

Remember, in the national park it is illegal to remove or pick vegetation. Leave the plants for the wildlife that rely on them and for other visitors like yourself to enjoy. There are lots of opportunities to collect plants outside the park, provided you follow some of these basic guidelines:

- collect only the plant part and amount you can use.

- if digging for roots, do so only in an area where soil erosion will not become a problem.

- don't collect rare plants or plants that do not appear abundant in that particular location.

- be positive about plant identification. Use the scientific name of the plant. It is not unusual for one plant to have several common names and this can lead to mis-identification. Some plants are very poisonous and the remote Nahanni is no place for mistakes!

Recommended Field Guides:

Porsild, A.E. **Rocky Mountain Wild Flowers** National Museum of Natural Sciences/Parks Canada 1974

Scotter, George W, & Flygare, Halle **Wildflowers of the Canadian Rockies** Hurtig Publishers 1986

Walker, Marilyn **Harvesting the Northern Wild** The Northern Publishers, Yellowknife 1989

Willard, Terry **Edible and Medicinal Plants of the Rocky Mountains and Neighboring Territories** Wild Rose College of Natural Healing 1992

Vitt, Dale H, & Marsh, Janet E, & Bovey, Robin B **Mosses, Lichens & Ferns of Northwest North America** Lone Pine Publishing, Edmonton 1988

Little, Elbert L **The Audubon Society Field Guide to North American Trees** Alfred A Knopf 1980

Common flowering plants of Nahanni

Scientific Name	Common Name	Colour – when in flower
Allium schoenoprasum	Wild Onion	purple, late June to July
Smilacina stellata	False Solomon's Seal	cream, mid-May to mid-June
Veratrum eschscholtzii	False Helibore	yellow-green, July to August
Zygadenus elegans	White Camas	creamy green, May to August
Calypso bulbosa	Venus Slipper	pink, late June to August
Corallorhiza trifida	Pale Coralroot	yellow-green, May to June
Cypripedium calceolus	Yellow Lady's Slipper	yellow, mid-June to early July
Cypripedium passerinum	Northern Lady's Slipper	white with purple dots inside, mid-July
Habenaria hyperborea	Northern Green Orchid	yellow-green to green with yellow, late June to mid-July
Habenaria obtusata	Northern Bog Orchid	greenish white, late June to mid-July
Orchis rotundifolia	Round-leaved Orchid	look like angels in purple dotted white robes with mauve hats and wings! mid-June to early July
Listera borealis	Northern Tway Blade	yellow-green, July & August
Spiranthes romanzoffinana	Lady's Tresses	white, July & August
Chenopodium capitatum	Strawberry Blight	red, July to August
Claytonia lanceolata	Spring Beauty	white to pale pink, late April to late June
Silene acaulis	Moss Campion	pink, mid-June to early August
Nuphar variegatum	Yellow Pond Lily	yellow, June to July
Aconitum delphinifolium	Monkshood	deep blue-purple, late June to July
Actea Rubra	Baneberry	white, late May to June
Anemone drummondii	Drummond's Anemone	creamy white, late May to late June
Aquilegia brevistyla	Blue Colombine	blue-mauve-purple with white trim, June to July

Common flowering plants of Nahanni — continued

Scientific Name	Common Name	Colour – when in flower
Delphinium glaucum	Tall Larkspur	deep blue-purple, mid-July to mid-August
Anemone patens	Prairie Crocus	pale blue to pale purple with yellow centre, late March to mid-May
Ranuculus eschscholtzii	Alpine Buttercup	yellow with green centre, late June to early August
Ranuculus gmelinii	Yellow Water Crowfoot	yellow, July
Papaver keelei	Poppy	yellow to orange, July & August
Drosera angelica	Sundew	white, mid-May to mid-July
Mitella nuda	Mitrewort	yellow-green stars, late June to mid-May
Parnassia fimbriata	Grass-of-Parnassus	white, July & August
Saxifraga aizoides	Yellow Mountain Saxifrage	yellow, June to July
Saxifraga cernus	Nodding Saxifrage	white, mid-July
Saxifraga tricuspidata	Prickly Saxifrage	white, late June & July
Amelanchier alnifolia	Saskatoon	white, late May to early July
Dryas alaskensis	Yellow Dryad	yellow, June to early July
Dryas integrifolia	White Dryad	white, mid-June to early August
Dryas punctata	Mountain Avens	white, mid-June to August
Frageria virginiana	Strawberry	white with yellow centre, June to July
Potentilla fruticosa	Shrubby Cinquefoil	yellow, late June to early September
Rosa acicularis	Prickly Rose	pink, purple, or white, late May to early August
Rubus acaulis	Cloudberry	white, mid-June
Astragalus alpinus	Alpine Vetch	blue, June & July
Hedysarum alpinus	Liquorice Root	pale pink, late June to early August

Common flowering plants of Nahanni — continued

Scientific Name	Common Name	Colour – when in flower
Lupinus arcticus	Lupine	blue to lavender, late June to early August
Epilobium angustifolium	Fireweed	pink, mid-July to late August
Epilobium latifolium	Broad-leaved Willow-herb	pink, mid-July to late August
Cornus canadensis	Bunchberry	white, late June to early July
Pyrola gradifolia	Arctic Wintergreen	pink, July to August
Pyrola secunda	One-sided Wintergreen	greenish white, mid-July to early August
Kalmia polifolia	Bog Laurel	pink, late June to July
Phyllodoce empetrifolium	Pink Heather	pink, July & August
Rhododendron lapponicum	Lapland Rose Bay	purple to pink, July to August
Androsace chamaejasme	Rock Jasmine	white, mid-May to early July
Mertensia paniculata	Bluebell	blue, late June to mid-July
Myosotis alpestris	Forget-Me-Not	blue, July
Castilleja miniata	Indian Paintbrush	red, yellow and white, June to late August
Veronica wormskjoldii	Alpine Speedwell	dark blue, July
Linnaea borealis	Twinflower	white to pale pink, late June to late July
Campanula lasiocarpa	Alpine Harebell	blue, July & August
Lobelia kalmii	Lobelia	blue to purple, mid-July to early August

Top left: Yellow Lady's Slipper (Cypripedium calceolus). photo: Gillean Daffern

Top right: White Camas (Zygadenus elegans).

Bottom left: Indian Paintbrush (Castilleja miniata). photo: Gillean Daffern

Bottom right: the rare Shooting Star (Dodecatheon frigidum).

Rare plants of Nahanni

Scientific Name	Common Name	Comments
Botrychium lunaria	Moonwort	found around Wildmint Hotsprings
Athyrium filix-femina	Lady Fern	found near hotsprings and in cool montane and subalpine areas
Cryptogramma crispa	Mountain Parsley	found on calcareous outcrops
Cystopteris fragilis	Fragile Fern	only found in two locations in the Mackenzie District
Dryopteris dilatata	Spinulose Wood Fern	
Dryopteris phegopteris	Beech Fern	
Matteuccia struthiopteris	Ostrich Fern	found on the flood plains of rivers
Pellaea glabella	Cliff-break	only found in three locations in the NWT, prefers neutral to acidic soils
Polypodium vulgare	Polypody	rare in the Mackenzie Mountains, prefers neutral to acidic soils
Lycopodium clavatum	Running Club Moss	
Potamogeton foliosis	Leafy Pondweed	rare in the south Mackenzie District
Potamogeton natans & P. pusillus Rupr.	Pondweed	rare in the Mackenzie District
Ruppia spiralis	Ditch Grass	found in the shallow water of Yohin Lake, disjunct from other areas – S Alberta, Saskatchewan, coastal Alaska
Festuca baffinensis & F. brachyphylla	Alpine Fescue	only two observations made in the area, prefers alpine tundra
Festuca rubra	Red Fescue	
Glyceria borealis	Boreal Manna Grass	restricted to S Mackenzie Mountains
Phragmites communis	Reed	found in a pond near Yohin Lake, only known site in Mackenzie Mountains

Rare plants of Nahanni — continued

Scientific Name	Common Name	Comments
Poa jordalii	unnamed grass	rare in Nahanni area
Carex interior	unnamed sedge	northern limit of range
Carex lachenalii	unnamed sedge	rare in Nahanni area
Carex macloviana	unnamed sedge	rare in Nahanni area
Carex williamsii	unnamed sedge	found in alpine meadows
Cypripedium guttatum	Lady's Slipper	only one found, in white spruce forest on an old flood plain
Habenaria dilitata	White Orchid	found at Hole-in-the-Wall Lake
Orchis orbiculata	Round-leaved Orchid	Spruce woods near the Rabbit-kettle River
Liparis loeselii	Twayblade	only location in NWT in on an island in Yohin Lake, in wet organic soil. The nearest other sample is 1450 km away — south of the S Saskatchewan River in Saskatchewan
Listera cordata	Heart–leaved Twayblade	only recorded in two sites in NWT, one at Hole-in-the-Wall Lake
Salix lasiandra	unnamed willow	
Sagina linnaei Presl	unnamed campion	rare in the Mackenzie Mountains
Ceratophyllum	Hornwort	Nahanni has one of two samples in NWT
Pulsatilla ludoviciana	Prairie Crocus	
Ranunculus pedatifidus	Northern Buttercup	
Drosera linearis	Sundew	
Chrysosplenium tetrandum	Golden Saxifrage	samples found near springs
Leptarrhena pyrolifolia	Leather-leaved Saxifrage	one of two samples in NWT

Rare plants of Nahanni — continued

Scientific Name	Common Name	Comments
Saxifraga adscendens	unnamed saxifrage	found in alpine
Saxifraga flagellaris	Spider Plant	found in alpine
Geum aleppicum	Yellow Aven	
Astragalus eucosmus	unnamed vetch	
Geranium richardsonii	Cranesbill	found in alpine meadows and near alpine streams
Viola adunca	Early Blue Violet	found in grasses of montane meadows and open forests
Viola pallens	unnamed violet	near hotsprings
Epilobium lactiflorum	unnamed willowherb	found in a hotspring meadow, Hole-in-the-Wall Lake
Pyrola minor	Lesser Wintergreen	rare in the Mackenzie Mountains
Moneses unflora	One-flowered Wintergreen	found in spruce woods at Hole-in-the-Wall Lake
Phyllodoce glanduliflora	Yellow Heather	rare in western Mackenzie Mountains
Diapensia obovata	Diapensia	found on acidic rocks, first record in the Mackenzie Mountains
Dodecatheon frigidum	Shooting Star	rare in the Mackenzie and Richardson Mountains
Lomatogonium rotatum	Marsh Felwort	
Scutellaria galericulata	Scullcap	
Mimulus guttatus	Monkey Flower	new record for the Mackenzie Mountains
Anaphalis margaritacea	Pearly Everlasting	nearest other sample 900 km away in BC
Antennaria campestris	Pussy-toes Everlasting	found on dry sites, montane
Antennaria nitida	unnamed everlasting	only occurs in the South Nahanni River area
Antennaria pulcherrima	Showy Everlasting	found in the alpine

Rare plants of Nahanni — continued

Scientific Name	Common Name	Comments
Arnica amplexicaulis	unnamed arnica	only samples in the Mackenzie Mountains
Aster franklinianus	unnamed aster	
Aster nahanniensis	Nahanni Aster	new species, found near Old Pot Springs, Wildmint Hotsprings
Erigeron yukonensis		rare in the Mackenzie Mountains
Heiracium albiflorum	Slender Hawkweed	
Senecio yukonensis		found in the alpine

Edible plants of Nahanni

Typha latifolia	Cattail	Below the waterline, the stem core and root shoots (best in spring) have a starch that can replace flour or be fermented to produce "hooch!" Dry the core, then pulverize it to get the starch without the fibres. The shoots can be eaten raw or cooked.
Montia sibiricus	Miner's Lettuce	The raw leaves, stems, and roots are all good eating in salad.
Hesysarum alpinum	Pale Sweetvetch	When raw, the root tastes like a mixture of coconut and peas; when baked, like potato chips; when fried, like parsnip. Caution: those with allergies, especially to fruit, may react violently.
Rosa woodsii	Wild Rose	Red rose hips are an excellent source of vitamin C, especially after the first frost. They may be eaten raw or cooked with soup etc.
Urtica gracillis	Stinging Nettle	The formic acid in this plant gives a nasty sting and rash. Fifteen minutes of boiling will remove the acid. Gather the tops when the plant is less than 15 cm tall and cook them in as little water as possible.
Epilobium angustifolium & E latifolium	Fireweed	The shoots can be boiled, the core of the stalk eaten raw, the flower head used to thicken stews, and the dried blossoms and leaves used for making tea (a good bush-bar mix!)

Edible plants of Nahanni — continued

Scientific name	Common name	Comments
Heracleum lanatum	Cow Parsnip	Before the flowers open, the stalks may be eaten raw. The skin of the stalks can give a rash and must be removed. The root can be cooked. Be positive of ID, it can be confused with the poisonous water hemlock!
Carex spp.	sedges	The core may be eaten raw cr cooked, May to August.
Phleum commutatum	Alpine Timothy	In fall, the heads can be stripped of seed, crushed, and made into a gruel.
Potentila anserina	Silverweed	In fall, the root can be eaten raw, roasted, boiled, or fried. The dried root has a nutty flavour.
Populus tremuloides	Trembling Aspen	Good from May to mid-July when the bark is easily removed. The cambium layer on the wood can be scraped with a knife to get a stringy fibre, sweet when eaten raw or dried. Also called Indian Spaghetti.
Pinus contorta	Lodgepole Pine	same as above
Viola spp.	Violets	The whole plant can be boiled like spinach
Ledum groenlandicum	Labrador Tea	The boiled leaves make a nice tea. Too much may give you a head or stomach ache.
Allium schoenoprasum	Wild Onion	Make sure the plant looks, smells, and tastes like an onion — it may be confused with Death Camus. Use all parts, year round.
Petasites sagittatus	Coltsfoot	Young leaves can be cooked like spinach. Leaves rolled tightly and burned to ash is a salt substitute.
Scirpus validus	Bulrush	The young shoots can be peeled, then eaten raw or cooked. The roots can be prepared like cattail, and the seeds ground to flour.

Medicinal plants of Nahanni

Scientific name	Common name	Comments
Arnica alpina	Arnica	the rhizomes and flowers can be used externally to stop the pain of bruises, sprains etc. They can also be used as a compress to relieve sore or black eyes.
Abies lasiocarpa	Balsam Fir	the resin found in bark blisters is good for minor burns. Cool the wound, apply the resin, cover with a light sterile dressing.
Populus trichocarpa	Balsam Poplar	buds can be used to make Balm of Gilead, a bitter tonic used to relieve digestive problems and headaches caused by liver or stomach disorders. One teaspoon of buds/cup of boiling water, 1-3 cups/day
Arctostaphylos	Bearberry	the leaves can be used to treat urinary tract inflamation and diabetes. One heaping teaspoon of leaves/cup of boiling water sipped throughout the day.
Petasites palmatus	Coltsfoot	a good cough remedy. 1-2 tsps of leaves and flowers/cup boiling water, steeped for 15 min. Drink hot several times per day. Young leaves and flowers can be eaten raw or cooked as a herb.
Rosa woodsii	Wild Rose	the red rose hips are an excellent source of vitamin C. Also a good diuretic.
Ledum latifolium	Labrador Tea	relieves coughs when used as a tea made from leaves. One teaspoon of dried leaves/cup boiling water. A tea made from the roots and bark can relieve skin rashes when used as a wash.
Equisetum variegatum	Horsetail	best source of calcium in the plant kingdom. Uses: flushes out the urinary tract, acts as a metabolic stimulant, relieves upset/ulcerated stomachs, reduces leg cramps, relieves pain from foot and leg injuries when used in a bath. It can also be used as a cold pack over sore muscles. Tea can be made from 1-2 tsp of stems/cup of boiling water, steeped for 15 min. Sip 3 cups/day.

Medicinal plants of Nahanni — continued

Scientific name	Common name	Comments
Heracleum lanatum	Cow Parsnip	found near hot springs. The young flower stems can be eaten raw or peeled and cooked. In the past, natives stuffed them with rice and cooked them. A tea made from the roots and seeds can help with a cold.
Epilobium	Fireweed	Helps relieve mucous congestion. One heaping tsp of root/cup water, boiled for 1/2 hr and taken in small sips over 1/2 hr, up to 3 times/day. The young shoots can be eaten like asparagus.
Valerian officinalis	Valerian	makes a good catnip for cats or sedative/relaxant for humans. One tsp of ground root/cup water, simmered 10 min, 1-2 cups/day. Relaxes stomach and bowel spasms, induces sleep. In cases of food poisoning, large doses will induce vomiting (a good defence against untalented camp cooks!).
Rubus idaeus	Raspberry	a nutritional herb, strong in citric acid and vitamin C. The tea is useful for female reproductive problems, cramps, colds, flu, children's diarrhoea, and as an eye wash.
Botrychium lunaria	Moonwort	Used as a tea, it was an ancient remedy used to stem the bleeding of internal injuries. Also good as an eyewash.
Potentilla fruticosa	Shrubby Cinquefoil	all parts of the plant can be used. One tsp/cup of boiling water may be used as a gargle for sore-throat, drunk for stomach cramps, or used as a skin wash.
Artemesia borealis	Wormwood	found on alluvial fans. Drunk as a tonic to aid digestion and cleanse the bowels.

Past Peoples and Early Explorers

Before the White Man

With the exception of some preliminary investigations, a comprehensive study of Nahanni's prehistoric record has not yet been completed. Based on the small amount and low quality of the artifacts found, archaeologists speculate that erosional processes and dense forest cover may be to blame for the general lack of findings.

However, from preliminary surveys we do know that a hunter-gatherer culture, using leaf-shaped spear points, may have been the first group of people in Nahanni, arriving between ten and nine thousand years ago. The most significant example of prehistoric occupation was uncovered at Yohin Lake where lithic artifacts indicate an intensive use of the area between 6,000 and 2,500 years ago |74*|. A site known as Chimney Point near Nahanni Butte Village possesses the best evidence of a historically extensive occupation dating forward to the 19th century [77*].

In 1986, Doug Eastcott, then Chief Park Warden of Nahanni National Park, discovered an arrowhead on Tlogotsho Plateau overlooking Deadmen Valley [78*]. Was this plateau used as a migration route through the Mackenzie Mountains during prehistoric times, or perhaps as a route south during the last ice age? An archaeological assessment was initiated to determine the significance of this fluted arrowpoint. The excavation of eight sites suggests that natives made use of Tlogotsho Plateau both before and after contact with Europeans. One notable discovery suggests that rocks were actually quarried for tools. There is also evidence that nearby mineral licks were used as bait for hunting.

The artifacts discovered during these excavations include:

- another fluted point
- a chi-tho (an implement used for to soften hides)
- end scrapers
- notched pebble sinkers used as weights to sink fishing nets
- a post-contact teepee ring with nails and pieces of tin can acquired through the fur trade

Although the discoveries made on Tlogotsho Plateau are inconclusive, they add fuel to suggestions that the plateau may have been used as a migration route between 10,000 and 9,000 years ago.

The Naha

The South Nahanni River is also called the Setting Sun River because it is the only river in this region that cuts through the mountains, disappearing into the sunset. Years ago this was the home of the Naha, which meant the People Over There Far Away, the Enemy, the People of the Setting Sun, the People Who Speak Like Ducks, or the Giant Enemy depending who was speaking of them. These people were also known as the Kaska tribe of the Nahanni Dene and were known to have travelled the local rivers using moose skin, birch, and spruce bark boats large enough to carry several families in each boat. It's believed they maintained a base camp on the Prairie Creek fan from which they staged their hunting forays.

The Good Giant Spirit, Ndambadezha, was the protector of these people. This great spirit was thought to inhabit the vent at the north mound of Rabbitkettle Hotsprings. It was said that, if the well was dry, bad luck would befall the people and, if overflowing, good luck was in store. Ndambadezha was credited with driving away the Great Beaver living atop Nahanni Butte which threatened to slap its huge tail and drown the people.

The Naha were said to have camped on Nahanni Butte, using the heights to help search for fires indicating camps that could be raided. Although they were a ferocious people, armoured with vests and shields made of closely tied sticks, their fierce reputation was not enough to keep most of them from being chased from the country by other natives in the 1880's.

Some intermarried with the Dene (pronounced dé-nay), a kind and peaceful people who presently occupy Nahanni Butte Village. Today, they still follow the traditions of hunting, trapping and fishing passed on by their forebears. Some continue to make moccasins, mitts and clothing in the traditional manner both for the tourist market and for their own use.

After the White Man's Arrival

The arrival of the North West Company at Fort Simpson in 1803 brought the first white man to the area. However, the rough terrain and treacherous rivers of the Nahanni prevented meaningful exploration until the early 1820's. In 1821, the North West Company dispatched the McLeod brothers to establish contact with the native people of the region and to forge a trading relationship. This relationship was established at Jackfish River in 1823 and at Meilleur River in 1824. Ultimately, a trading post was built in 1904 near the present location of Nahanni Butte Village. The amount of trading activity in this region quieted significantly when it was learned that

List of Cultural Sites

#	Description	Location
62	historic cabin site	NW end of Rabbitkettle Lake
63*	worked stone fragments	Rabbitkettle Lake
64	remains of Fred Sibbeston cabin	N bank of Flat River 3 km above the confluence
65*	unknown base camp, tent platforms, pits, artifact scatter	35 km upstream on the Flat River, W bank
66*	bi-face stone tool and bone fragments	above Irvine Creek mouth
67*	fire-cracked rock, bone fragments	downstream from Irvine Creek mouth on the Flat River
68*	Albert Faille cabin	upstream from Irvine Creek mouth on Flat River
69	partially subterranean cabin, had sod roof	clearing adjacent to Wildmint Hotsprings
70*	collapsed platform cache	upstream of Deadmen Valley cabin
71	cabin site of Mathews and Patterson	E bank of Sheaf Creek at South Nahanni confluence
72*	possible native occupation site, grave, stumps	downstream of Kraus Hotsprings
73*	cabin sites of Field, Lafferty brothers, other prospectors. Old scow probably Gus Kraus's	opposite Kraus Hotsprings on the South Nahanni River
74*	prehistoric sites with rock and animal remains and evidence of woodworking	Yohin Lake & area
75*	single bi-face stone tool	Nahanni Butte — parkside
76*	animal remains, evidence of hunting	W bank of Liard River below Chimney Point
77*	extensive occupation site lasting over several centuries	Chimney Point on South Nahanni
78*	prehistoric and historic site, may be evidence of prehistoric migration route	Tlogotsho Plateau
79	Jack LaFlair's cabin and grave	under Nahanni Butte on N side of South Nahanni River

* identifies features within a general area rather than a specific location

the South Nahanni did not provide an easy route over the mountains into the Yukon, and this, along with intertribal feuds and a limited fur supply, caused the North West Company and its associates to focus their attention on the Liard River instead.

The people of the Nahanni area, now well established in the fur trade, became increasingly dependent upon white culture. Natives began to assume more permanent settlement at Fort Liard and Fort Simpson, partly to seek medical help for those who had fallen sick from diseases brought by the white man.

In the 1870's, the Canadian government began to take more interest in the resources of the north. The Senate Committee concerned with the Greater Mackenzie Basin recognized the significant development potential of the area's forests, fur, minerals, and agriculture, and it suggested the government maintain a greater presence in the north in order to control the use of these resources. At the time, Nahanni's own resources were considered relatively insignificant.

The Yukon Gold Rush of 1898 created the first significant interest in Nahanni. A few gold-hungry travellers came looking for an alternative route to the Klondike. Others, after having had no luck in the Klondike, came into Nahanni from over the continental divide via Ross River, but by and large there was still very little interest in the region. Then tales of gold, reportedly found by Willie and Frank McLeod up the Flat River, began to raise hopes for a second Klondike. In the end, Nahanni gold was found in only small quantities in 1922, 1929, and 1933.

Those few who ventured into Nahanni returned with tales of horror and mystery. Most significant was the discovery of the headless bodies of Willie and Frank in Deadmen Valley in 1908 and the bullet-riddled body of Martin Jorgenson up the Flat River at Irvine Creek in 1915, a grisly find which Poole Field thought was connected in some way with the fate of the McLeod brothers. Nahanni's mystique was compounded by the rumoured deaths of many would-be Klondikers at the river's headwaters where giant natives, ruled by a woman of part European ancestry, committed evil deeds. A prospector named John O'Brien was found atop Twisted Mountain frozen to his core. Another man by the name of Shebbach, died of starvation, and four others simply disappeared. Bill Eppler and Joe Mulholland vanished near Glacier Lake in 1937, Phil Powers never returned to the cabin on Irvine Creek, Andy Hall was last seen walking up Scow Creek on his way to the Flat River and, most heart rending of all, a young girl named May Lafferty went missing up the Flat River during a hunting trip. One prospector blew himself up with dynamite, while numerous others drowned in the whitewater. Not surprisingly, Nahanni was popularized as a place that could deliver either incredible riches or horrific death.

Imagine sitting by your campfire during a quiet evening in Deadmen Valley

photos: Phillip Godsell courtesy Glenbow Archives

Willie (left) and Frank McLeod, victims of the curse of the Nahanni.

and staring up at the vibrant northern lights that stretch across the northern sky. Were these ghostly sheets of light also enjoyed by the McLeod brothers before they parted with their heads? Good night and sweet dreams!

Some Nahanni Pioneers

Jack LaFlair (or LaFleur) competed with the Hudson's Bay Company through his trading post at Nahanni Butte from 1915 until his death in 1950. During my Nahanni days I lived in what once served as his store and log house, but since then the warden station has been abandoned due to erosion of the river bank, the age of the buildings, and the possibility of the Butte collapsing during the next earthquake. Jack's grave lies alongside one of his cabins at the northeast end of the station in the bush [79]. Dick Turner took over the trading post after LaFlair's death.

Albert Faille, 1888-1973, was a longtime explorer, trapper, and prospector of the Flat River area mainly, although he did travel far above Virginia Falls on several occasions. An excellent documentary film of his exploits, made by the National Film Board of Canada, is available for viewing at the park office in Fort Simpson. This film will make you think twice before wimpering over your troubles on the Virginia Falls portage! One of Albert's cabins remains standing beside the Flat River near Irvine Creek [68*].

Gus Kraus Three years younger than Albert Faille, Gus Kraus came into the

207

Top left: Gus, Jennifer and Mary Kraus (1985).
photo Doug Eastcott

Bottom left: Albert Faille with photographer's
daughter Diane Beckett (summer 1973).
Photo Don Beckett.

Top right: Dick Turner (1985).
photo Doug Eastcott

Bottom right: R.M. Patterson (left) and Gordon
Matthews (Spring 1946). Photo courtesy British
Columbia Archives & Records Service # HP65777

Nahanni area in February 1934 to prospect for gold. He established himself at Kraus Hotsprings in 1940 and was joined two years later by his new bride, Mary. Together they remained at the hotsprings until 1971. Gus, a prospector and explorer, was made an honorary game warden for the Nahanni area, even though he had once served a three month sentence in Hay River for trapping game without a licence. He assisted the RCMP with their investigation of the mysterious McLeod brother deaths. He adamantly believed that a mining engineer named Wier had joined the brothers in the search for gold and was responsible for their deaths.

I met Gus and Mary at little Doctor Lake in 1985. At 85 years of age, Gus was still full of "piss 'n' vinegar" as he reminisced over his life. I remember one tale in which he related how "the army" in Alaska had on one occasion mistaken the wind direction while experimenting with incendiary balloons, causing them to crash in Nahanni and start a few forest fires. On taking my leave, I remember how anxious Gus was to return to work on the construction of their new log cabin. He still believed there was gold on Marengo Creek — the dream never dies! He died in Fort Simpson in 1992 at the age of 92.

Raymond Patterson Both Patterson and Albert Faille first visited Nahanni in 1927. In fact, they were travelling companions for some of the time. Patterson's incredible journey took him from Fort Simpson to Virginia Falls, then up the Flat River to the headwaters of the Caribou. His trip finished with a paddle up the Liard to Fort Simpson and a 100 mile overland hike to Fort St. John!

Patterson returned with Gordon Matthews the following winter to trap for furs in Deadmen Valley. On one occasion, worried about the overdue return of Matthews by dog sled, Patterson, equipped with tarpaulin and light blanket, travelled down the partially frozen South Nahanni to the Liard and on to Fort Simpson by snowshoe. A tough haul for anyone, but especially in temperatures plummeting to below - 40 degrees Celcius.

Patterson produced the first map of the area and wrote "The Dangerous River", a book which served to sharpen the interest of many an adventurer.

Dick Turner Dick Turner practised a number of professions in the Nahanni area including trapper, gold prospector (using Patterson's map), river-man, trader, magistrate and bush pilot. In addition he authored three books on the north: "Nahanni", "Wings of the North" and "Sunrise on Mackenzie".

His adventures began in 1930 when he and his brother Stan left Alberta to trap for furs on the Netla River. The idea was to make money for schooling, but Dick fell in love with the north and decided to stay. He and his wife Vera set up home on the bank of the Liard River close to Lindberg Landing, after having lived at Netla River for ten years. For a while they also operated a trading post under Nahanni Butte, which later became the warden station until it was abandoned in 1988.

Two pages overleaf: Where the adventure began: the upper South Nahanni near Moose Ponds.

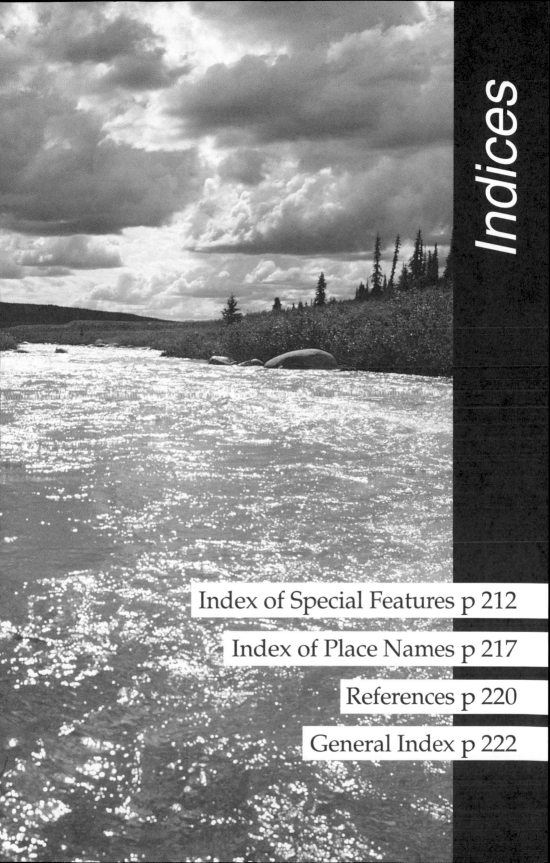

Indices

Index of Special Features

Index of Special Features — continued

#	Subject	Location	map #
21	glacial spillways	Mary River, May Creek, Fishtrap Creek	17,21
22*	interlinking glacial scour troughs and solifluction sheets incised by glacial marginal channels, globally unique feature	Hole-in-the-Wall Valley	10
23	ice-moulded bedrock with anastomosing meltwater channels, rare in Canada	downstream of Flood Creek	13
24*	highly weathered glacial till including erratics from the Canadian Shield, rare in this region of Canada	Nahanni Plateau & Lafferty Creek	20,21
25	horned peak	Hole-in-the-Wall Valley	10
26	U-shaped alpine glacial valley	Rabbitkettle Valley	10
27	periglacial feature, solifluction lobes	throughout the Nahanni area	13,14,16,19, 20,25,26
28*	glacial marginal meltwater channel cut in bedrock containing small karst sinkholes, a rare combination	near Hell Roaring Creek	12
29	glacier breached divide	throughout the Nahanni area	12
30*	proglacial lake floors a) of second glacial lake Nahanni b) Glacial Lake Tetcela	a) Caribou River b) Deadmen Valley & Clausen Creek	19,20,21,27
31*	intensively dissected 1st & 2nd Glacial Lake Nahanni deposits	Flat River confluence	16,17,28
32	kame & kettle features	N end of Yohin Ridge on river left	21
33	terminal moraine of the Laurentide Ice Sheet	Mattson Mountain	22
34	consequent canyons, outstanding Canadian example	Lafferty Canyon	20,21

Index of Special Features — continued

#	Subject	Location	map #
35	antecedent canyons –	Third Canyon	17
36	best examples in	Second Canyon	18
37	Canada	First Canyon	20
38	cut-off meander, unique global feature	The Gate	18
39	fluvial landform	Pulpit Rock	18
40	Virginia Falls	Virginia Falls & Fourth Canyon	14,15,16
41	slanted bedrock, enormous rapids	Sluice Box	14,15,16
42	alluvial fan	Prairie Creek	19,20
43	silt plug	Prairie Creek	19,20
44*	rotational slumps	Sunblood, Deadmen Valley & Clausen Creek areas	14,19,21
45	The Great Spur – regular, in-growing river entrenchment, 1320 m deep; a well-developed and globally unique feature	Second Canyon	18
46	fluvial landform, cut-off meander, regular asymmetry due to steady growth. Is now a separate 425 m-high mountain, uniquely well developed in a global context	First Canyon	20
47	bedrock terracing with in-growing and in-trenching canyon development, no other example in Canada	Third Canyon	18
48	fluvial landform, dolomite badlands, outstanding example in national context	Prairie Creek Canyon	19,20
49	fluvial landform, unconstrained river meander channels	Rabbitkettle & Jackfish Rivers	10,22
50	fluvial landform, alluvial fan	Flood Creek	12
51	fluvial landform, multiple river terraces	Irvine Creek, Caribou River & E of Yohin Ridge	21,22,25,26,27
52*	periglacial feature – patterned ground / frost polygons, best example in the park	south mound of Rabbitkettle Hotsprings & Tlogotsho Plateau	8,9,10,11,19,20

Index of Special Features — continued

#	Subject	Location	map #
53*	periglacial feature – patterned ground / frost stripes	The Gate	18
54*	periglacial feature – thaw ponds	throughout the area	8,10,11,12,13
55	karstlands drainage	Whitespray Spring	20,21
56*	karstlands, among the best examples in the world	N of First Canyon	20
57	karst feature – Grotte Valerie cave system, unique in global context	First Canyon	20,21
58	pseudokarst feature – Rabbitkettle Hotsprings, only known large tufa mound hotsprings in Canada, possibly in the world at this latitude	on Rabbitkettle River	8,9,10,11
59	pseudokarst feature – piping sinkholes, some of the best known examples in Canada	Rabbitkettle & Yohin Lake areas	8,9,10,11,21,22
60	mineral licks for Dall's sheep	across from Sunblood patrol cabin, Deadmen Valley — upper fan, river-left 1/2 km before George's Riffle, across from Kraus Hotsprings	14,19,20,21
61	glacial scoured lakes	Irvine Creek	12
62	historic cabin site	NW end of Rabbitkettle Lake	8,9,10,11
63*	worked stone fragments	Rabbitkettle Lake	8,9,10,11
64	remains of Fred Sibbeston cabin	N bank of Flat River, 3 km above the confluence	16,17,28
65*	unknown base camp, tent platforms, pits, artifact scatter	35 km upstream on the Flat River, W bank	25,26
66*	biface stone tool and bone fragment	above Irvine Creek mouth	25,26
67*	fire-cracked rock, bone fragments	downstream from Irvine Creek mouth on the Flat River	25,26

Index of Special Features — continued

* identifies features that are within a general area

Index of Place Names

Bennett Creek	origin unknown. Formerly known as Gold Creek.
Blackstone Landing	translated from Slavey "burned little stones".
Brintnell Creek	named after Wilfred Leigh Brintnell, President of Mackenzie Air Service Ltd. Pilot of the Harry Snyder expedition to the Nahanni in 1934.
Caribou River	descriptive, origin unknown.
Cirque of the Unclimbables	named for vertical walls of the mountains which challenge expert climbers.
Clausen Creek	named after Ed Clausen who trapped at the river mouth in the 1920's.
Clearwater Creek	descriptive, Albert Faille called it Murder Creek, referring to Martin Jorgenson's death.
Deadmen Valley	named by Poole Field around 1907 after finding the headless bodies of the McLeod brothers.
Direction Mountain	likely named by bush pilot Wop May in the 1930's. Used as a landmark to the supposed gold fields of the Flat River.
Dry Canyon Creek	descriptive, origin unknown.
Flat River	Dene name "White Boiling River".
Flood Creek	descriptive, origin unknown.
Funeral Range	after plane crashes which killed several bush pilots and passengers .
George's Riffle	after George Sibbeston who had a near miss here early in the century.
Glacier Lake	descriptive, origin unknown.
Grotte Valerie	named by French spelunker who first explored cave.
Haywire Lake	name supplied by Dwight Herbison of Tungsten, 1974 as a name in local use.
Headless Creek, Range	after the murdered McLeod brothers. Their camp was near this creek.
Hole-in-the-Wall Creek, Lake	descriptive name supplied by G.C.F Dalziel, of Dease Lake, BC. Officially accepted form is un-hyphenated.
Honeymoon Lake	likely named after newly-weds John and Joanne Moore.
Irvine Creek	origin unknown, Slavey name "the joining of the waters".
Island Lake	descriptive, origin unknown.

Index of Place Names — continued

Index of Place Names — continued

Prairie Creek	refers to tundra at headwaters known as Caribou Flats. In Slavey "river of the clearing formed by forest fire".
Pulpit Rock	named by R.M. Patterson because it resembles a church pulpit. Gus Kraus called it the Gate Post.
Rabbitkettle River, Lake, Mtn, Hotsprings	translates to Rabbit Pot. The legend states the waters were so hot people cooked rabbits in it.
Ragged Range	after rough appearance of the topography.
Ram Creek	after the abundance of Dall's sheep in the creek.
Sheaf Creek	named by R.M. Patterson after a Wheat Sheaf pub in England.
Seaplane Lake	named by bush pilot H.A. Doc Oakes. In 1928 he was the first pilot to land on the headwaters of Flat River.
Secret Lake	origin unknown.
Sluice Box	after the device used to prospect gold.
Sunblood Mtn.	named by Daniel the Flying Trapper who commented upon the colour of the mountain, especially at sunset. The site of two plane crashes; one in 1968 resulted in the death of all aboard.
Swan Point	descriptive, origin unknown.
Tlogotsho Plateau	translated means "big place of grass".
Twin Falls	after a water fall which splits into two after hitting a ledge.
Twisted Mtn.	descriptive. Previously called O'Brien Mountain, it was renamed by a government geologist exploring oil and coal potential in 1949. Dene name translates to "something big pushing up, emerging".
Virginia Falls	named in 1928 by American explorer Penlay Hunter after his daughter Virginia.
Whitespray Spring	after the appearance of the water.
Wildmint Hotsprings	after the wild mint which grows around the springs.
Wilson, Mount	named in 1909 after Charles Wilson, prospector.
Wrigley Creek, Whirlpool	after Hudson Bay Company steamer "Wrigley" which plied the waters of the Mackenzie River.
Yohin Lake, Ridge	after Denes Charles Yohin and his father who trapped in area. Also known as Jackfish lake.

References

Addison, W.D. **Nahanni National Park Historical Resources Inventory Parks Canada, Volume 4, A Preliminary Chronology.** W.D. Addison & Associations, Kakabeka Falls 1976.

Anon. **Nahanni National Park Reserve, Resource Description and Analysis** Natural Resource Conservation Section, Parks Canada, Prairie Region, Winnipeg, Manitoba 1984.

Anon. 1992 **Explorers' Guide** Travel Arctic, Government of the Northwest Territories, Yellowknife, NWT 1992.

Banfield, A.W.F. **The Mammals of Canada** University of Toronto Press. 1974

Binns, J. & R. Moorehead. **Nahanni: Historical and Visitor Survey** Parks Canada, Western Region 1973.

Carbyn, L.N. & D. Patriquin. **Description of the Wildlife Component for Impact Assessment of Three Potential Campsite Locations in Nahanni National Park, NWT.** Unpublished Canadian Wildlife Service Report, Edmonton 1978.

Chadwick, D. H. **Nahanni: Canada's Wilderness Park** National Geographic. vol.150, no.3, September 1981.

Ford, Derek **Strange Landforms of the South Nahanni** Canadian Geographical Journal February/March 1977.

Gadd B. **Handbook of the Canadian Rockies** Corax Press, Jasper 1986.

Hanks, C. **A Pass to the South: Anatomy of a Traditional Route Across the Tlogotsho Plateau, Mackenzie Mountains, NWT.** Canadian Parks Service. Unpublished document, Yellowknife, NWT 1991.

Harding, L. **A Canoeist's Exploration of Nahanni Park** Canadian Geographic. vol. 100, no.3. June/July 1980.

Hartling R. Neil. **Nahanni: River of Gold ... River of Dreams** Canadian Recreational Canoeing Association 1993.

Jeness, D. **The Indians of Canada** (6th ed.) National Museum of Canada. Bulletin 65, Anthropological Series No. 15 1963.

Kochanski, M. **21 Native Wild Edible Plants of the Spruce Moose Forest** unpublished document.

Mackay, R. **Status Report on Trumpeter Swan (Olor bucinator) in Canada** Committee on the Status of Endangered Wildlife in Canada 1978.

References — continued

Mason, B. **Path of the Paddle: An Illustrated Guide to the Art of Canoeing** Key Porter Books 1984.

McKown, D. **Canoeing Safety and Rescue** Rocky Mountain Books, Calgary 1992.

Miller, F.L. Caribou. In: **Wild Mammals of North America: Biology, Management, and Economics** J.A. Chapman and G.A. Feldhamer (Eds), John Hopkins Univ. Press, Baltimore 1982.

Miller S.J., N. Barichello and D. Tait. **The Grizzly Bears of the Mackenzie Mountains, NWT.** NWT Wildlife Service Completion Report. No. 3., Yellowknife 1982.

Moore, J. R. **Nahanni Trail Head** Deneau and Greenburg, Ottawa, Ontario. 1980.

Ogilvie, W. **Exploratory Survey as part of the Lewes, Tat-On-Puc, Porcupine, Belly Trout, Peely and Mackenzie Rivers Part VIII,** Annual Report, Canadian Department of the Interior, Ottawa 1899.

Patterson, R. M. **Dangerous River,** Stoddart. Reprint 1989 (hbk), 1992 (pbk).

Scotter, George W. **White-tailed Deer and Mule Deer Observations in Southwestern District of the Mackenzie Mountains, NWT.** Canada Field Naturalist 1974.

Skinner, M.F. & Kaisen O.C. **The Fossil Bison of Alaska and Preliminary Revision of the Genus. Bull** American Museum Natural History 1947.

Soper, J.D. **Mammals of Wood Buffalo Park, Northern Alberta and District of Mackenzie** J. Mammal, Journal 23: p 119-145 1942.

Turner, D. **Nahanni** Hancock House Publishing, Saanichton, BC 1975.

White, W. E. **The Birth of the Nahanni: Nahanni Beguli** Environment Canada-Parks. Microfiche Report Series.

Wickstrom, R.D. & Lutz A. **Tungsten and Copper Analysis of Fish and Sediments from the Lower Flat River, Nahanni National Park** Canada Wildlife Service Manuscript Report 34p 1981.

Youngman, P.M. **Notes on Mammals of Southeastern Yukon and Adjacent Mackenzie District** National Museum of Canada, Bulletin No. 223: p 70-86 1968.

Note: Field Guides are listed in the relevant chapters

General Index

Index — continued

Index — continued

about Peter Jowett

Peter has been with the Canadian Parks Service since 1981 when he worked as a park ranger in Alberta and as a canoeing instructor/guide for the Ontario Ministry of Natural Resouces. Since joining the warden service in 1984 he has worked all over western Canada including a two year stint in Nahanni — his favourite park. He is currently stationed at Pacific Rim on Vancouver Island.

For more years than he can remember, Peter has been plying the waters of Canada from Ontario to the Yukon, first solo, then with his wife Judy and now with his newborn son and future bowsman Dawson Alexander.